HERMITAGE

HERMITAGE

A Place of Prayer
and Spiritual Renewal:
Its Heritage and Challenge
for the Future

JOHN MICHAEL TALBOT

Crossroad · *New York*

1989
The Crossroad Publishing Company
370 Lexington Avenue, New York, N.Y. 10017

Library of Congress Cataloging-in-Publication Data

Talbot, John Michael.
    Hermitage: a place of prayer and spiritual renewal : its heritage
and challenge for the future / John Michael Talbot.
        p.   cm.
    Bibliography : p.
    ISBN 0-8245-0901-3
    1. Hermitages.   2. Eremitic life.   3. Spiritual life—Catholic
authors.   I. Title.
BX2845. T35   1988
255′ .02—dc19   88-25868
                                                                     CIP

CONTENTS

v

INTRODUCTION

We live in an exciting era—a time when many Christians are experiencing a powerful call from the Spirit radically to live the gospel of Jesus Christ and to help reconcile all creation to the harmony and love of our heavenly Father. The Second Vatican Council called all religious and spiritual communities in the church to rediscover the roots of their own particular charism, and to live that particular charism authentically in today's world. By following that call, religious communities can better fulfill their particular roles in the united Body of Christ and bring the challenge of the gospel of Jesus Christ to the world of the future.

This book is written for the four hundred and fifty or so religious congregations of the Franciscan family already in existence, and for those who do not yet exist except in visionary fire that burns within a solitary heart. It is also for those of other monastic and religious families who seek to integrate some dimension of the shared eremetical tradition within the lived experience of their own particular organization today. Holding this tradition in common, we are already joined together in a seraphic community of the Spirit that transcends all legal lines or barriers. In addition, I hope that *Hermitage* will be of some value to those Christians seeking to build lives of action on a firm foundation of contemplative prayer.

A hermitage is the habitation of a person who chooses to live in seclusion for a period of time for spiritual reasons. It can be modern or ancient, furnished or spare, in the desert, the woods, or the city. Where it is or what it looks like is not the point; what is important is that a hermitage be a place of prayer and spiritual renewal. The purpose of this book is to rediscover that early and authentic Franciscan charism called "Franciscan eremitism," and to suggest some future applications based on past learnings. It is my hope that this book can encourage all of us to stay true to whatever charism is unique to our own congregation or vocation while building our future upon that which we all share in common in the spirit of Christ.

Francis of Assisi, influenced by the spirituality of the desert fathers and seeking the authentic fire of the gospel and example of Jesus, lived a great part of his own religious life in solitary prayer within a hermitage. It is from the hermitage that we usually see Francis venturing forth to renew the world in the power of the Holy Spirit which he himself had first received after long hours of intense mystical prayer. It is a fact that most of the events which we popularly associate with Francis of Assisi took place either in or around a hermitage, and either during or after a time of intense solitary prayer in union with Christ. The powerful Franciscan apostolates that renewed the face of the Western world literally sprung from this individual and communal emphasis on an intense life of prayer. It is owing to this fact of history that most successive renewals and reforms of the Franciscan family have included a strong renewal of both individual and communal prayer along with a childlike openness to the gifts of the Holy Spirit and intense mystical union with Jesus Christ, our divine lover and our Lord.

It is a fact of Franciscan history that whenever there has been an emphasis on reaching out in evangelism to the active world, it has always flowed forth with power from a primary emphasis on charismatic and contemplative prayer, as experienced within the communal environment of the Franciscan hermitage or "house of prayer."

Today, as we look into the renewal within the religious and Franciscan families, we see another strong emphasis on outreach. But while our emphasis is on world hunger, global peace, and social justice—all vitally important aspects of the authentic Franciscan life—we must also balance this external ministry with a proper understanding and experience of interior mystical union with Jesus Christ. It is the power of the Holy Spirit that brings a balanced experience of the gospel of Jesus Christ, causing it to spread like an unquenchable fire throughout the world. To achieve this balance, we Franciscans need to foster a communal environment that is conducive to deep contemplative prayer and mystical union with Christ. In this sense every Franciscan house must be a "hermitage" or house of prayer, and I believe that the more intense expression of the hermitage should be more accessible and prevalent than it is in today's communities. Only then will our individual and communal outreach gain its full potential as an undeniable spiritual force within our world. Consequently, a new look at the Franciscan eremitical life is once more needed if we are to understand both the structures and the flexible freedom that this life requires and fosters, and thus come to establish and live this life in a way that is balanced and mature.

The Franciscan hermitage exists only to bring a person into union with God. It would be a tragic error unduly to see the hermitage as an answer to all of one's spiritual needs and problems, and then subtly emphasize the structure of a physical place and way of life over simple union with Jesus. The Franciscan hermitage can subtly become an "idol" that a frustrated brother or sister can mistakenly worship. It is Jesus we must worship, and Jesus we must follow! Just as Francis of Assisi sought to live and proclaim the life of the gospel, so must we seek the direction of Jesus and his gospel as we now discern how to apply the Franciscan eremitical life in a developed way to the varied situations of individuals and communities in today's world. Let us not seek to overly legalize or externalize a life that exists for the purpose of interior union with Jesus. Let us seek the scriptural and historical guides that will aid and protect a gospel life that is free in the wind of the Spirit. I believe that a balanced study of the basic facts will provide us with a proper historical flexibility to aid and guide us toward this goal in today's complex world. I hope that this book will be of some help to others in bringing further spiritual power to the current renewal of the Franciscan family and the church, so that all the world might be renewed in the loving gospel of our Lord Jesus Christ.

PART I

The
Past

1

THE TRADITION OF
THE DESERT FATHERS

T he spirituality of the Franciscan hermitage is born in the mountains and in the woods. It is not really a spirituality of the desert. In this the underlying spirituality of the Franciscan hermitage is vastly different from that of the desert fathers.

Almost all of the places Francis chose for hermitage sites are situated in the mountains. The mention of woods and rivers are frequent, as also are the wide array of nature scenes alive with wildlife, colorful foliage, and flowers. While the spots might be removed enough for the solitude of eremitical living, they were never so far removed from the towns and villages that the friars could not easily go out among the people to beg and to preach.

However, this does not mean that Franciscan eremitism shares nothing in common with the eremitism of the desert. The need to integrate solitude and community brings about a similarity in the basic physical outlay of both the *skete* or *laura* of the desert eremites and the "places" of the Franciscan hermits. Both sought out a more rugged natural environment, unaffected by the luxuries of the city. Both experienced the "dark nights" of the soul as they encountered the pure spiritual darkness within their own soul and sought to bring it into the redemptive love and light of Jesus. Also, it must be admitted that the monastic reformers of the West who so affected the religious environment from which Francis came were all intentionally seeking to integrate the spirituality and lifestyle of the desert fathers into the lush mountains and deep woods of Italy, France, and throughout Europe. It was primarily the natural environment that was different.

At the beginning of almost any discussion of the history of Christian eremitism, one must respectfully begin with the tradition of the desert fathers of the Christian East. Early and primitive as it is, this Eastern tradition is rich in both the disciplined rigor and the flexible wisdom that formed the healthy womb from which almost all future forms of Christian religious life in both the East and the West should be born and grow. Francis's life, and the lives of those who followed him in the Franciscan movement, are no exception. So any complete study in Franciscan community should include at least some mention of the desert fathers.

This is especially true in the study of the life in the Franciscan hermitage, for it is this aspect of the early Franciscan lifestyle that most genuinely reflects and resembles the pure tradition of the Christian hermits of the East. It is evident that Francis's mixed form of a solitary life of prayer and apostolic work, unique as it was in many ways, was nonetheless influenced in at least an indirect way by the informal and flexible eremitical life of the desert hermits of Egypt, Syria, and Palestine.

As we know, Francis was directly influenced by the many new contemplative communities of the eleventh and twelfth centuries of the Gregorian reform. We also know that it was the intent of these communities of the reform to reintroduce the radical gospel life of prayer and poverty of the early desert fathers' tradition into the developed and sometimes lax religious life of the Christian West. However, they sought to do this in a new integration that was creative and sensitive to the spiritual needs of their own time. Consequently, it was probably through the direct influence of these new contemplative communities of the Gregorian reform that Francis was at least indirectly influenced by the pure hermit tradition of the deserts of the Christian East.

We can see this influence in almost every dimension of the Franciscan hermitage. Following the other religious reformers of his day, Francis also sought to integrate seemingly opposite concepts and forms of Western religious life into a working universal whole that simply manifested the whole of the life of Christ as depicted in the gospels. From the perspective of the gospels, these integrations seem very natural for a person who seeks to follow the example of Jesus and his disciples without compromise. Thus there are integrations between strict solitude and a family-like community within the Franciscan hermitage. The family quality of community brings an integration between necessary structures and desirable freedom and flexibility. Consequently, there are further integrations between informal and formal prayer, both in private and in community. Even beyond these, there are the seemingly revolutionary integrations between contemplation and action that make the "Franciscan mix" a rather difficult and novel thing to explain, much less to live.

Most of these gospel integrations seemed unreasonable and outrageously "untraditional" to the highly institutionalized and structured forms of a more limited monasticism that had developed in the West. In fact, some of these integrations seemed to threaten the very foundation upon which the formal religious life of the Christian monks of the West built their entire institutional system. This is not to say that all Western monasticism of that period was by its authentic nature "bad," for all these "novel" integrations of Francis and other reformers are clearly manifested in the traditional simple life of the hermits of the East, from which the monasticism of the West was actually born. Western monasticism simply needed to be reformed by being called to return to its gospel roots. So Francis of Assissi, along with other new monastic founders and foundresses of the Gregorian reform, actually sought to strengthen the foundation of a truly catholic monasticism by reestablishing the gospel simplicity and flexibility of the Eastern desert fathers within the little mountain hermitages of the Christian West.

The two greatest "fathers" of the desert were St. Antony (c. 251–356) and St. Pachomius (c. 290–c.346). There were other greats from both sexes, but these two stand out as great founders. They both lived in Egypt. They lived at the same time. Yet, they represent two radically different approaches to monasticism. Later generations integrated these two approaches into one.

St. Antony was a hermit. He based his life on the same gospel verses that inspired St. Francis. With this inspiration he went into the desert to seek God alone. He attracted disciples quite unintentionally as the Spirit brought them. Only then did a sort of community develop. They developed a leadership and occasional common meetings for conferences and prayer. But this was loose-knit and occasional at best.

Physically the individual hermit cells were scattered at random around a few common buildings. Solitude was a priority, so very little community building or structure was needed. Other great examples would be St. Macarius of Scetis (c. 300–c.389) and Evagrius Ponticus of Wadi Natrum (c. 346–399), both in upper Egypt.

St. Pachomius is the father of the cenobitic life. This is a definite life in common, patterned after the Jerusalem community of Acts 2. In contrast to the hermit life, he envisioned the brothers living, working, and praying in common daily. A definite leadership and structure thus developed under Pachomius.

In the beginning the words "monk" and "hermit" were used interchangeably. The word "monk" comes from the Greek *monos,* which means "alone." Originally, the monk was one who adopted the eremitical or hermitical life as envisioned by St. Antony. The monk was a hermit.

The cenobite was one who lived in community. He was not considered a monk because he did not live alone. He lived with brothers. Ironically, as time passed the use of the words was reversed so that the monk was considered the cenobite and the hermit was not considered a monk. This occurred primarily in the Christian West after the widespread use of the overtly cenobitical Benedictine rule. But in the beginning the hermit was considered a monk. The one who lived the common life was considered a cenobite, not a monk.

I have never visited the monastic ruins of Egypt, but I have had the privilege of visiting some sites of early monastic foundations of hermits in the Holy Land. In places such as St. George's monastery in the Wadi Kelt, between Jerusalem and Jericho, it is an awesome thought to ponder the fact that where now dwell only eight monks and one hermit, there once dwelt eight thousand monks and hermits! The arid desert of Palestine literally burst forth into a glorious monastic flower that was rooted deeply in the waters of eternal life. To this day the steep, rocky walls of this dried-out riverbed are solidly lined with miles of small inaccessible caves that once served as hermits' cells. In the midst of this desert where Jesus was led into solitude by the Spirit to be tempted by the devil, an actual city of monastic hermits flourished in a time when such foundations became quite common in Egypt, Syria, and Palestine.

What strikes one most, as one studies the written hermit tradition of the Christian East, is again the Spirit-led and living flexibility that characterizes the life of the early desert fathers. Seeking only to be followers of Jesus, these first monks and hermits did not make an idol or god of a monastic structure. These structures existed only for the sake of aiding the Spirit-led gospel life of prayer and poverty that these men and women sought by following Jesus in worshiping the Father. God alone was to be worshiped! Consequently, the full example of Jesus Christ and the inspiration of the wind of the Spirit always took precedence over the human monastic structure. Likewise, the Spirit-led life of the community and the living guidance of spiritual fathers were always the basis of "the rule," used to deal with the structural reality of a prayer community which had been charismatically dealt with in the beginning. In fact, most communities did not even bother to write down their "rules." Rather, they chose to write down the spiritual discourses of their spiritual fathers regarding deeply spiritual things. This is what they wrote when they wrote at all. Even then it was mostly visitors from the outside who wrote the dialogue and conferences of the first charismatic leaders of the monastic life. Such was the case of St. John Cassian (c. 360–c.435), who wrote two famous works on early monastic life, the *Institutes* and the *Conferences*. Only much later in history was it necessary to write "monastic rules." Thus the "monastic rule" evolved from living experiences before becoming a legal reality.

From the writings we now possess, we know that some formal structure did exist, however, from the beginning. Under the inspiration of the Spirit, and under the guidance of a spiritual father and a council of elders, we see that these desert communities came to some mutual agreement regarding basic spirituality and schedule. In order for a community to pray together, work together, or talk together on any kind of a regular basis, some schedule and structure had to be developed. Yet in these structures and schedules we always find both the zealous seriousness and the flexibility that should characterize any living community of the Spirit which seeks to follow Jesus to the heavenly Father without compromise.

It seems that with the unfolding of years in the desert tradition, a classic pattern began to develop regarding the integration between solitude and community. This classic pattern involves a "three-level" system, allowing various degrees of solitude within a community. This system can still be witnessed in Mt. Athos today. The first level was the *cenobium*, or the large monastic "city" where a regular common life of prayer and virtue was lived in nearly constant close company with others. The second level was the *skete* and *kellion*, or small family-like monastic "village" or "cottage," where the semieremitic common life was lived with more flexibility in common discipline and where much more time was allowed for private prayer in solitude. The third level was the strict hermitage, or the hermit living temporarily or permanently in solitary reclusion, separate, yet united with other hermits, and juridicially attached to a monastery.

The young monk on Mt. Athos today usually begins to live the common life in the larger *cenobium*. Only after proving himself worthy in the charity and love involved in living the gospel life of prayer and poverty with others is the maturing monk allowed to go to the small *skete* to concentrate more on solitary prayer and deeper personal relationships. When the monk is fully mature in the first two levels he is allowed to go into strict seclusion, if he feels God is calling him to this life.

Ironically, the very first monks and hermits of the desert began in an almost opposite pattern. Usually a lone hermit lived many years in solitude before attracting disciples. When others joined the hermit, he would live a more semieremitic lifestyle with his young companions in order to instruct, guide, and teach them intimately. Many followers would then themselves go into the desert after spending several years with spiritual fathers. Often they too went on to attract followers, thus beginning the cycle all over again. It is at this point of the cycle that we begin to hear about most of the founding fathers of the hermit colonies of the desert. Only after a great many followers came to the desert, or tried to live this life elsewhere, was a more cenobitic monasticism developed in order to apply more moderately the harshness of the solitary desert life to the communal and temporal needs of the average person. This is the case especially with the cenobitic Pachomian monasticism of Egypt.

Owing to a pluralism in both structure and pattern, the classic pattern is lived in a variety of ways in the East today. The prospective hermit may be received directly into the *skete*, without living first in the *cenobium*, if it is obvious from the beginning that he definitely seeks the eremitical life rather than the cenobitic life. Likewise, those who do not seek the more difficult eremitical way of life may enter the cenobitic monastery with no obligation to go to the *skete*. However, if a cenobitic monk feels a call to solitude, he will sometimes go on to the *skete*, or may even pass directly to a solitary hermitage attached juridically to the monastery. Likewise, a monk may choose to enter into the *skete* directly and never pass on to the strict solitary hermitage without feeling any guilt. He has no obligation to become a recluse. In all this, great care is taken by the spiritual director and the community to seek the authentic spiritual good of the aspiring monk or hermit. Thus we can see great spiritual freedom exercised in applying the "classic pattern" of the East.

Nevertheless, some training in community and under a spiritual director is universally required before the strict solitary life may be entered into. Therefore, the Spirit-led freedom and pluralism of the East should not be seen as a license to do whatever you like whenever you like in the name of Christ. The authentic life in the Spirit is always seen as a communal reality, even when dealing with the call to solitary prayer and lifestyle.

In addition to a freedom in living out the classic pattern of the eremitical East, there also seems to be great structural freedom regarding both the actual organization and the government of this way of life. Sometimes one will find a cenobitic monastery with individual hermitages attached directly to it, without the existence of the semieremitical *skete*. In these cases, the hermits are directly responsible to the abbot and council of the *cenobium*. In return the cenobitic monastery is responsible to support the isolated hermit. One can also find solitary hermitages attached to a *skete* in a similar arrangement, yet the *skete* itself may be totally autonomous from any cenobitic monastery regarding both government and physical support. Yet one will never find a solitary hermit who is not attached and accountable to some community or who does not live under the approval and good graces of the overall monastic community which represents the desert fathers' tradition in today's world.

As stated before, the leadership of the community is also a flexible and living reality. In the beginning the charismatic leadership of the spiritual father served as the primary judicial "rule" for the *skete*. There was little separation between the charismatic and the legal realities of communal leadership. Only with the passing of many years did those in legal leadership sometimes cease from being the primary spiritual fathers of the eremitical community. With the accumulation of administrative responsibilities, it sometimes became impossible for the abbot truly to be a spiritual father. So it soon became common to separate and then to integrate the governmental leadership of the abbot and the personal spiritual leadership of the spiritual director. They were seen as "two yet one." However, this separation did not always happen; so a simple understanding of the abbot as a spiritual father was often retained.

Furthermore, with the various relationships between the *cenobium*, *skete*, and the solitary hermit, leadership over one or the other varied. In the strict classic pattern the formal abbot of the *cenobium* is the final juridicial leader of both the *skete* community and the individual hermit. However, in the case where the *skete* is autonomous, the more informal spiritual father is the charismatic leader of both the *skete* and the isolated hermits. Again, no hermit is left totally "on his own."

The commitment of the individual monk was, again, a very informal matter with the desert fathers. The simple reception of an

aspiring hermit seemed to be nothing more than a mutual understanding of strict obedience to the spiritual father. Later, the clothing
of the aspirant in the monastic habit seemed to be an informal sign
of the hermit's obedience to God and his spiritual father. From the
writings of John Cassian and the stories of the desert fathers, we
receive an indication that some form of commitment was made, but
it was not until monasticism found its way West in the *Rule of the
Master* and the *Rule of Benedict* that we see any kind of solemn
ceremony surrounding the promise of obedience. It was not until
the time of the mendicant friars of the West that the official "vows"
of poverty, chastity, and obedience became necessary for the
church's official recognition of the "religious state." The earliest
Christian councils are unclear on this matter. The concepts of private
and public vows, along with their precise legal character, seem to
be a much later development of the post-Gregorian reform and post-
Innocent III church of the tenth to thirteenth centuries. In the West,
all later understandings hinged on these later developments, thus
making a further proper development sometimes very difficult. It
does seem ironic that the very founders of monastic life would not
have been officially recognized as monks by the church after the
time of Pope Innocent III (1160–1216)!

The liturgy of the desert-father tradition also shows great flexibility. It seems that common prayer and eucharistic worship range
in frequency from daily, to weekly, to monthly. Weekly Eucharist
seems to be the moderate norm that prompted the recitation of the
psalms in the "divine office" as a form for daily common worship.
Yet some communities did not even gather for daily common prayer,
feeling the life of solitude and informal and spontaneous shared
prayer to be more important. The internal structure and frequency
of the divine office seems to have varied from place to place, thus
giving rise to the "monastic liturgy" and the individual liturgical
rites of various monastic communities. There seems to have been
a great freedom regarding the use of scripture and their order or
place in the divine office. There was a further freedom regarding
the *way* the divine office was prayed; it was sometimes sung of
recital, either individually or together. New studies of the monastic
liturgies of the East also indicate that much of the common prayer
of some communities was spent in silent meditation, leaving but a
small portion of the common prayer period for any reading at all.
Their use of scripture was indeed very free regarding the order and
the way it was used. Usually the psalms were taken in the biblical
order rather than in the "thematic" way of the cathedral liturgies.

Likewise, one or two hermits would often do all the reading or sing-ing, thus preserving the "meditative" character of the prayers. Only later does the entire community begin to read or sing the psalms together. Of course, as the mature hermit entered more intensely into solitude, he was often given yet more freedom to remain in his cell rather than going to the church for common prayer.

The above freedom and flexibility do not mean that there was no discipline or rigor. On the contrary, we find both the private and communal prayer disciplines of these first hermits to be more than what most modern monks could endure. Though communal prayer might have been infrequent, its internal quantity was high. All 150 psalms were often prayed in common daily, and often repeated in private. Thus, the scriptures were almost always in the monk's mind, for memorization was the primary tool for teaching scripture to a community that often did not possess a Bible. Likewise, the sac-ramental mystery of receiving the Lord with the church in Eucharist was always seen as a central dimension to the authentic hermit life, as long as this liturgy did not destroy the rhythm of the hermit's solitude when celebrated communally, and as long as a subtle cler-icalism did not bring pride into the community through this em-phasis.

The private discipline of the monk was also a highly flexible yet an extremely intense reality. Mortification in fasting, vigils, food, clothing, shelter, and work, plus repetitive scriptural prayer, all en-tered into the regular daily life of the hermit; yet no universal "law" can be found as to how every monk should have exercised personal discipline. It seems that some graduation in intensity from moderate to extreme was involved in every area of personal discipline, thus apparently involving the intimate, personal guidance of a spiritual father. From the later example of one like Gregory of Sinai (d. 1346), we receive an overview of a tradition in which some say a hermit should have six hours of sleep, some say four, and some say the "perfect" need not sleep at all! Some allow changes of clothes for washing and for cold weather, some allow only one rough tunic for all times of the year. Some eat moderately, some eat hardly anything at all. Yet in all these things, a discernment of the individual spir-ituality and endurance of the hermit is involved, thus allowing a seemingly great flexibility in hearing God's voice regarding personal discipline.

A final integration and flexibility can be seen regarding contem-plation and action in the tradition of the desert. Within the very idea of a "spiritual conference" or "dialogue," where spiritual fathers speak the wisdom of God to younger monks, one can see the concept of "apostolic ministry" at work within the hermit community itself. It seems that these conferences were rather informal, though it seems some scheduling was possible. Some commentators believe the monks met three times a week for conferences with their elders. Beyond this we do have the examples of some hermits and monks who went on either formally or informally to minister to the church and the world. Antony himself was known to preach to the crowds when the survival of the church was at stake.

The integration between celibate communities of men and women is not totally lacking from the tradition of the fathers either. We see from the work of Palladius in his *Lausiac History* of desert monasticism that female hermits or anchoresses were somehow included in the desert *sketes* and the Pachomian double monasteries of the East. How this worked out in practical details is sometimes vague, but we do at least know that they were there. There were also many monasteries of women attached to the towns and villages of the East. Later, during the time of St. Jerome (c. 347–419/420), we know that double cenobitic monasteries of monks and nuns also existed in the Holy Land on Mt. Olive and in Bethlehem. These were very similar to the double monastery of St. Benedict's (480–546) day in the West, keeping a rather strict separation between the men and the women. We do know that an emphasis on proper separation of the sexes was prevalent in both the canon law of the church and in the informal attitudes and practices of the early hermits themselves. This attitude is itself a reaction against the practice of celibate men and women living in community as brother and sister. No doubt, several abuses within this lifestyle created scandal in some places. Yet the "scandal" of these "co-ed" households could have been nothing more than the evil minds of the onlookers. When anchoresses were present in the desert hermit colonies of Egypt, it is possible that the seclusion of the daily hermit's life provided separation enough between the sexes. A further development of this male/female integration of the East took place in the North during the peak of the success of Celtic monasticism, which is one of the most pure developments of the early desert-father tradition outside of the East. In Celtic monasticism, rather free integrations between men and women took place in both the structure and in the government of the "hermit colony," with both abbots and abbesses governing a double monastery.

It would be a great mistake, however, to assume either that there was so much freedom that zealous discipline and fervor were not centrally important, or that some of the later particular developments of the West were unjustified. On the contrary, we know that the desert tradition of the East is one of the more rigorous ascetical traditions of Christian monasticism. It does seem ironic that when the most structural freedom was evident in the monastic communities, there was usually a great charismatic move of the Spirit, who called men and women to a personal holiness that was voluntary. Owing to abuses against the Spirit of God and to further proper definitions of the work of the Spirit of God, many structural disciplines properly developed to guide and protect the monastic communities. Also, it should be understood that strong charismatic leadership preceded a primitive, legal structure, thus making the legalities less important for the immediate survival of the community and making the lifestyle much more flexible. It should not be understood that a loose, informal structure will cause a move of the Spirit. When the Spirit is moving, however, a loose, informal structure is more likely to succeed. It seems that in the West some developments were often overly legalistic and have sometimes proven a hindrance to developments that are needed in modern times to face the challenges of the future. Francis of Assisi often faced the same problem in his own time as he sought to return to the original ideal of both the desert and the gospel of Jesus Christ.

2

EARLY ASCETICS, VIRGINS, AND ITINERANT PROPHETS

᪣

Thus far we have emphasized the semieremitic desert fathers of Egypt, but we should also, at least briefly, mention the ascetical communities of early Syrian and upper Egyptian Christianity. These communities did not emphasize the solitary life as strongly as did the desert fathers' *skete* or *kellion*. They definitely represent a more active and cenobitic approach to community life. Nonetheless, they influenced the overall development of intentional communal and monastic forms of life in the Christian West, to which Francis of Assisi most certainly belongs.

Let it first be said that the ascetical community tradition represents a more biblically oriented heritage than does the more culturally novel hermit-like approach of the desert fathers. The Qumran community of the pre-Christian and Christian Jews definitely introduced a nearly monastic approach to community life to the Jewish people of Israel. They themselves drew heavily from the prophetic and eschatological tradition of the Old Testament which saw schools of prophets gathering around a highly charismatic figure such as Samuel or Elijah. Their concept of solitude and asceticism, consequently, took on a "separatist" prophetic flavor that adapted easily to their highly eschatological outlook toward the "world." This asceticism included not so much a self-sacrificial understanding of service-oriented self-denial, as it did a highly practical approach to being free of entrapment to the world's system, and a ritual cleanliness that affected diet, ritual washings or baptisms, and social conduct in general.

The later Judeo-Christian ascetical communities worked from a very similar understanding. The separatists' approach to asceticism continued as they looked for the return of Jesus to be the eschatological event to take place in their own lifetime. Gospel poverty could be seen as a highly practical ideal that freed the Christian community from the material dependency on the world's system which was passing away. Baptism and even Eucharist could be seen as retaining many of the Jewish flavorings that went along with many of the ritual washings of the Essenes of Qumran and the Passover of the Mosaic people of the Exodus.

Yet these early communities also drew from the Hellenized strand of Judaism in both their structure and in their overall spirituality. Adapting the approach of the philosophical schools of Antioch and Alexandria, these early Christian ascetics approached poverty and study in ways that ironically represent the very culture from which they were trying to separate. For the philosophical school, poverty became a means of remaining free from an overly physical dependency on the culture to whom they were trying to minister. Furthermore, it did represent the willingness to "die" to one's self-oriented needs in order to serve the world and enlighten the world with true Mind. Likewise, study, knowledge, and contemplation were ways to discover this "Universal Mind" and the ways "Universal Mind" could benefit the world.

For the early ascetical schools, these translated very easily into Christian thinking. The philosophical school's approach to poverty coincided greatly with both the Jewish ascetical teachings of Qumran and the teachings of Jesus. The redemptive concept of the cross of Jesus Christ was seen as the true completion of the philosophical school's concept of self-sacrificial poverty. Like the philosophical schools of Antioch and Alexandria, the Christian communities saw the need for study, mediation, and contemplation of both scripture and secular philosophy and science if ministry to the passing secular world was to be fully effected. It should be noted that active ministry was very much the "end" toward which contemplative and meditative study was seen only as a "means."

It has been pointed out by scripture scholars that of the four gospels, St. Luke's most accurately represents the Syrian ascetical approach to living out the gospel of Jesus Christ. Luke emphasizes the self-sacrifice of poverty much more strongly than do the other three gospel accounts, making poverty an almost mandatory manifestation of taking up the cross of Jesus. Yet the "Hellenized" approach of the "Gentile physician" also places a strong emphasis on not only knowledge of Jewish scripture, but also on a highly contemplative appreciation of God's revelation through all creation and the universal dimension of God's saving grace in Christ. The solitary dimension of the Christian life is emphasized primarily through Luke's account of Jesus' life on earth, yet never to the exclusion of his active ministry.

It is both Luke and Paul who emphasize the "higher call" of both celibacy and the common life, not to mention that both Paul and Luke seem very familiar with the Hellenized traditions of the philosophical schools, as well as the Jewish eschatology and ascetism of Qumran. Likewise, we see in Paul's life an emphasis on solitude at the beginning of his conversion, yet never to the exclusion of his apostolic mission. It is the gospel tradition of both St. Luke and St. Paul that forms much of the "biblical" or apostolic footing upon which the building of early Christian ascetical community would rise.

As both St. Paul and St. Luke emphasize the virtue of celibacy for both virgins and widows, loose-knit Christian communities of brothers and sisters soon began to form. These communities took shape as separate households of men and women, and also "mixed" communities of sorts existing among Jesus' first disciples. The practice of men and women living together under one roof as celibate brothers and sisters was generally looked upon as scandalous by both the church and the world. This was probably due to actual abuses of this practice in both Christian and non-Christian celibate circles, plus an unfortunate tendency for human beings to assume the negative and gossip about things that are purely figments of the imagination. Nonetheless, while the practice of such "mixed" communities seemed to convey successfully the informal expression of gospel celibacy for a few years, it was the segregated tradition of separate households of men and women that eventually prevailed and was accepted as "orthodox" by all for the coming generations.

St. Paul speaks of the "order" of virgins and widows in his letters, thus tracing their origins to the very beginning of the church. Ignatius of Antioch (d. shortly after A.D. 110) and Cyprian of Carthage (d. 258) also speak of this order of virgins. There is evidence of their existence in both the Middle Eastern and North African expressions of Christianity. Apparently this order was comprised of individuals who lived in their own homes rather than in formal community. Only with the development of continent marriages, or marriages without sexual activity, did these ascetics and virgins begin living under one roof. Apparently, some "mixed" households also developed among nonmarried ascetics and virgins. This practice was formally stopped by the Council of Nicaea, but no mention of sexual immorality ever occurs. The church was opposed to the self-mutilation and castration often practiced in order to guard against sexual immorality. The only other negative comments come from both Ignatius and Cyprian who warn against the spiritual pride that often accompanied those consecrated to God through the order of virgins.

Also related to this movement are the itinerant prophets. Both the *Didache* and the *Ecclesiastical History* of Eusebius (c. 260–c.339) mention their presence in the early church. Apparently, these charismatic figures wandered like the first apostles, living a life of austere asceticism and preaching to the early church communities. They worked alongside the more stabilized and stationary apostolic structure of the local churches, thus building the church on the scriptural foundation of both the apostles and the prophets with Christ Jesus as the cornerstone as described by St. Paul. The *Didache* would suggest that these itinerant prophets celebrated the Eucharist freely in union with the local bishops.

Undoubtedly this was not without its problems. The *Didache* warned against itinerant prophets freeloading off the local church for more than three days without working. They were to be considered false prophets and asked to move on. The abuse of the charismatic gifts in general within the church undoubtedly cast a further shadow on these Spirit-led itinerants. Paul's first letter to the Corinthians deals with such abuse. The rise of the charismatic heresy of Montanism dealt a new deathblow to any blanket acceptance of the more charismatic dimension of the church from the fourth century onward. Only in the Christian tradition of the pilgrim will we see this tradition kept alive, at least in part. During the Gregorian reform these pilgrims will again exercise the rather self-appointed office of itinerant preacher.

These itinerant prophets have a direct influence on our study of a hermitage that is Franciscan. The time immediately preceding St. Francis was full of itinerant hermit-preachers and pilgrim-prophets. As before, these charismatic individuals were sometimes saints and sometimes well-meaning heretics who caused much trouble in the church. St. Francis was himself a charismatic itinerant. He used the hermitage as a place in which to pray and from which to set out on mission. The genius of St. Francis was his ability to reconcile the charismatic with the structure once more. He raised up the prophetic alongside of the apostolic again by working with, rather than against, the clergy of the church.

As a movement of the universal Spirit of God, the entire tradition of ascetics, virgins, and itinerants grew up spontaneously and developed alongside the eremitical tradition within the church. These two communal traditions began independently, yet must be seen as complementary expressions of the same movement of the Spirit. As these contemplative communities' expressions grew and spread throughout the church, they were often integrated into a working whole as the same originating Spirit guided the proper and harmomious development of the church. This is especially true as the overall tradition of the Christian East moved into the Western world of the late Roman Empire. Consequently, we see both the formal monastic and informal penitential communities of the Christian West integrating the concepts of solitude and community, contemplation and action, male and female, etc., in a wide variety of ways that all trace back to legimate communal expressions of early Christianity. As we shall see, it is a reform approach to these developed forms of Western monastic and penitential community that so radically shaped both the person and the religious culture of St. Francis of Assisi. Even the more active tradition of the early ascetical Christian communities has a great deal of relevance to a balanced study of fully integrated Franciscan hermitage.

3

CELTIC MONASTICISM

❧

Ireland was once known as the "Isle of Saints and Scholars." It was on this island that the early Celtic monks and hermits gave themselves to mystical prayer, the study of the scriptures, and a lifestyle radically changed by the gospel of Jesus Christ. It was from the witness of their radical gospel lifestyle that eventually all of Ireland, Scotland, Northern England, and much of Continental Europe would be converted to Christianity. St. Columba of Iona (521–592), St. Brigid (c. 456–c. 524), and the popular St. Patrick (c. 385–461) are among many names that bring spiritual and historical honor to this holy island.

During the tenth, eleventh, and twelfth centuries, the holy Celtic monks and itinerant hermits wandered through Italy on pilgrimage to the Holy Land. Consequently, they had a substantial impact on the religious environment that helped to shape the vocation of St. Francis of Assisi. Between the influence of the desert fathers of the Christian East and the influx of pilgrim monks from the Christian North, Francis of Assisi developed a new integration of traditional spirituality that centered on mystical prayer and gospel poverty that allowed the friars to live the life of contemplative prayer and itinerant wandering as hermit-preachers. It was their living example and their powerful words that affected the major renewal of the thirteenth and fourteenth centuries which would sweep through the entire Western world.

The similarities between early Celtic monasticism and early Franciscan eremitism (life in the hermitage) are very profound.

Some of the early Celtic stories about the monks and hermits greatly resemble the *Little Flowers of St. Francis* in their emphasis. Both indicate a childlike wonder at God's work in creation, even down to the smallest of creatures such as birds, insects, and worms. Both bring out the humorous and human qualities of the real people involved in the legends and stories, such as the good-hearted Brother Juniper. And both manifest an emphasis on poverty that makes sense only in light of the divine, mystical love for the real human person of Jesus, the Incarnate Word of God.

It was this emphasis on the simplicity of the gospel of Jesus Christ that gave the early Celtic monks the same flexibility as the early Franciscan hermit-preachers to alternate between a primitive and uncluttered life of prayer and a life of wandering from village to village to preach the good news of the Father's kingdom under the divine inspiration of the wind of the Holy Spirit. It was this Spirit-led gospel flexibility that gave the mystical power to their prayer and lifestyle, which in turn caused the spread of this holy fire through every region they visited and every vicinity they came to inhabit.

Historically, a mystical flexibility has often characterized not only the Irish Franciscans and early Celtic monks, but the entire early Celtic church in general. The organization of the local church was often left very much up to the discretion of the local bishop. However, since the evangelization of Ireland came primarily from the monks, the episcopal seat of a diocese was often connected to the local monastery. In fact, the local bishop would sometimes be a monk of the local monastery. Consequently he would be under obedience to the abbot in all things except expressly ecclesial and diocesan affairs. It is even more surprising to learn that the bishop-monk was sometimes a member of a double monastery of monks and nuns where a nun was the abbess and the superior of the entire monastic foundation. In the case of St. Brigid of Kildare, the local bishop was a monk of a monastery that was governed by a woman! It is a fact of history that even though this arrangement sometimes created power struggles, it was in the midst of this period of Spirit-led flexibility that the faith of Ireland soared to a zeal of fever pitch that led to the evangelization of all the land.

The early Celtic and Franciscan flexibility in the midst of faithful obedience has much to say to the church of today's world. In particular, the flexibility between contemplative cloister and active mission, between proper structure and Spirit-led freedom, has much to say to the new expressions of Christian monasticism that must be developed as we meet the challenges of our immediate future.

The early Celtic "monasteries" were composed of a small group of primitive huts or "cells" centered around a small chapel. They were often arranged in three circles moving outward from a center. The center circle would be an area for the monks, the middle circle would be the area for the nuns, and the outer circle would be for families. All were considered "monks" and all lived in obedience to the abbot or abbess. In some cases the abbot or abbess could actually be a member of the family-oriented group. The buildings were made of stacked stone, built without the more modern invention of mortar. This is seen especially in the beehive huts of Skellig Michael, the Gallerus Oratory, and the round tower of Aghado. The "cloister" consisted of nothing more than a ditch or a primitive wall around the perimeter of the complex. This arrangement is very similar to the informal eremitical colonies of the hermits of Palestine and Egypt. Between the witness of history and archaeology this indicates a flexible integration on many levels.

While making room for intense lives of solitude and silence, these colonies were still designed so as to function in both work and worship as a community. There was a very real integration between solitude and community on one level. Furthermore, while emphasizing the contemplative life and separation from the world, they had no strict "cloister" in the medieval sense of the word to keep them from venturing forth to evangelize and minister the gospel of Jesus to the world. On another level there existed a very real integration between contemplation and action. While emphasizing the childlike simplicity of the gospel message and lifestyle, the monks were still very much involved in advancing the cause of holy study and secular, higher education among both the clergy and the laity. Thus, another level of integration existed in the holy mix of gospel simplicity and the study of God-given wisdom. Owing to these flexible integrations, these holy places of solitary prayer frequently had great impact on the local region in which they were situated, often becoming centers for evangelization and learning, or even becoming the episcopal seat of the bishop of the diocese.

Both the individual and the monastic community were centered emphatically on the simplicity of mystical union with Christ through an emphasis on individual meditation or contemplative and common liturgical prayer. These holy monks, whose lives were centered on both knowledge and experience of Christ's presence, could be driven by the wind of the Spirit to bring the message of the gospel of Jesus Christ to all the world. A spiritual flow from solitude to community and from contemplation to action was always possible. The emphasis was always on prayer, but the spiritual action that flows from prayer was never stifled. Consequently, a powerful move of Spirit-led evengelization spread like wildfire across the land.

We must rediscover this message as Christians and Franciscans today. The more recent tradition of medieval monasticism has a tendency to emphasize contemplative community only within the context of strict cloister. Likewise, the active communities of the more recent past have a tendency to emphasize primarily the apostolic dimension of the gospel to the exclusion of proper time or space for individual and communal contemplation and meditative prayer. Both of these extremes, when taken as the pattern for all Christian communities, have proven to be tragic misinterpretations of the older and more authentic traditions of our monastic and communal roots as fully universal or Catholic Christian.

As we face the challenges of the future, we need Christian communities rooted deeply and primarily in prayer that leads to an openness to mystical union with Christ, yet communities accessible to and concerned with the needs of the common people. We need communities of men and women who take time to hear God's voice in silence so they can come to know how better to proclaim his word to a world polluted by noise. We need communities of men and women who allow themselves to be touched tenderly by the recreating action of the Spirit, so as to bring more creatively the gospel of Jesus Christ to a world already saturated by the commercialized versions of pseudoart and half-truths.

The Franciscan hermitage was, and still can be, a place ideally suited to this purpose—a place where creative silence, creative liturgy, and creative lifestyle can be discerned and nurtured in the apparent rhythms of the Spirit. As we study more deeply our early historical sources, we come to discover a firm foundation upon which we can build these creative communities of prayer in the future. As we look more deeply into our beginnings, we find sure patterns of renewal that, contrary to being archaic voices from the past, prove to be incredibly relevant to the issues facing us today.

When we look to the spirituality and lifestyle of the early Celtic monks and hermits, we cannot help but see a great similarity to the early Franciscan movement. As we seek to understand more fully the charismatic and historic roots of our own Franciscan past, we cannot help but seriously study the Celtic monks whose pilgrimages to the Holy Land, at least indirectly, influenced the vocation of Francis of Assisi. The similarities are too evident to be ignored.

The Celtic church was a monastic church. It was not patterned after the normal Roman model prevailing in most churches of Continental Europe. This is traceable to the way in which the Celtic church was founded.

Most people recognize St. Patrick (385–461) as the founder of Christianity in Ireland, even though Palladius was sent by Pope Celestine I as a missionary before Patrick in 432. Patrick was born in Daventry in Britain, the son of a deacon and the grandson of a presbyter. He was apparently taken prisoner by Irish pirates and sold as a slave to a Druid. After repenting over his wasted and sinful years as a youth, he escaped to England in 407. He felt called by God to convert Ireland to Christianity, but first is said to have possibly lived for years as a monk in Gaul at Auxerre or Lerins.

Palladius brought a distinctly Roman Christianity to Ireland, while Patrick's was more British. Patrick's version was more monastic, even though it was still more episcopal (oriented to the urban diocesan model). Both versions, however, were considered more Roman-oriented than the monastic structure that would prevail later for centuries. Although both came first, they met with failure or limited success when compared to the more monastic model of later founders and saints.

Several cultural factors were involved: the existence of the clans, the Druids, and the bards. The clan was the basic structure of Celtic society. Instead of living in cities, the Celts lived in tribes or clans. There were many settlements, ruled by a family head, but there were simply no big cities. This made it very difficult to superimpose a diocesan episcopal structure based mainly on the concepts of the city, state, or Celtic territory.

The Druids were the holy men and women of the ancient Celtic religion. Nothing was formally written about this mystery cult, so little is verifiably known. We do know, however, that these mystical figures lived both in loose-knit communities and as solitaries. They were the main religious leaders of the Celts. That fact also made the highly organized and logical episcopal structure of Europe very unnatural for the Celts.

The bards were the traveling poets, harpists, and singers of the people. They alone were seen as the scholars of the land, and they roused the national awareness and conscience of the Celtic people in time of conflict, trial, or war. The settled episcopal structure of Rome could not compete with these itinerant troubadours who so won the sentiments and love of the people.

The monastic church was, however, well-equipped to meet and embrace these challenges. The monastic model harmonized well with the structure of the clan, for each monastery was but a small settlement for God. The monks of the monastery were often blood-related, and the offices of abbot and abbess were almost always passed on through a blood-succession within a family or clan.

The lifestyle of the mystical Druids also resembled the lifestyle and spirituality of the charismatic monks; so the people were more comfortable with this style of Christian leadership. Likewise, the solitary dimension of the Christian hermit monks strongly resembled the way of life of the Druids. The episcopal bishops did little to win the mystical respect of the people. Furthermore, the pilgrim-hermit monks who wandered as missionaries resembled the loved and respected bards. The monks were scholars, and their semi-eremitical settlements soon became centers of learning for the Celts, despite their small colony-like structure.

Patrick himself was a monk trained in the Continental European pattern, yet he did not found full-blown monastic settlements in Ireland. He tended toward the more Augustinian or Ambrosian ideal of a house of apostolic workers who gathered together to support one another in their ministries. It is not the monasticism that would flower later. Patrick also supported the virgins and ascetical women who lived in their own houses or grouped together into loose associations, but he never founded anything close to the great example of Brigid of Kildare or Hilda Whitby.

The actual monastic founders came about one hundred years later, in the sixth century. Finnian (d. 549) was the first of the monastic founders, from whom all the other greats would flow as disciples. Ciaran established Clonmacnois on the Shannon in 545 after Finnian founded Clonard in 515. Comgall established Bangor on the southern shore of Belfast Loch in 555–559. The famous Brendan established Clonfert in 558 or 564. It is St. Brendan who is said to have set sail from his hermitage near Galway with some of his disciples to look for more solitary spots. Some say this took him as far west as Iceland, Greenland, and even Newfoundland. The also famous Columba established Durrow, Derry, and Iona in the same century. It is the so-called "rule" of Columba that became the legislation for all Celtic monasticism for centuries to come. All practiced a form of semieremitical monasticism that stands as the most unique and most integrated form in all of history. Also of great renown is Columban (c. 543–615), who ended up going to Gaul and on into Bobbio in Italy to spread the influence of Celtic monasticism throughout all Europe before it was absorbed into the Benedictine observance under Benedict of Aniane in the tenth century. Still, the Celtic monastic observance stood as the unquestioned leader in both integration and holiness throughout Europe for almost three hundred years.

There were tensions between the Celtic and Roman models of Christianity, even though the Celtic monks never sought to break from the pope in Rome. The Celts held the Johannine date for Easter along with Eastern Christianity, and so were in tension with the Roman liturgical calendar. Likewise, the Celtic tonsure differed from the Roman; so there was a visible difference in the appearance of their respective clergy and/or monks. Furthermore, the monastic-based church of the Celts tended to make their missionaries in Gaul and Italy less than sensitive to the diocesan clergy and bishops. Consequently, many Celtic monks were persecuted when they migrated to Continental Europe. This reached a head when Columban had to appeal to Rome for the pope's protection of his way of life when he began founding monasteries throughout Gaul and even as far south as Bobbio in Italy.

Also of great importance are the female Celtic virgins and ascetics, or nuns. The greatest of them is, of course, St. Brigid of Kildare (c. 460–528). She founded a double monastery for monks and nuns living under the same Celtic rule. Their cells were in separate areas, but they all came together in one church for prayers, where the men and women were separated by a high wall. Although the monks were technically under Abbot Corlaed, Brigid was the undoubted leader and bore the title "abbess" over the whole complex. Although this sounds very segregated by modern standards, the integrated nature of such a double monastery was revolutionary for its time. Its emergence and success caused it to become a common pattern for Celtic monasticism for centuries.

Another great woman who adhered to this Celtic model of monasticism was St. Hilda (d. 680), although she lived in what we now call England and is claimed by the Benedictine family. St. Hilda was raised in a royal family who were among the first Christian families in England. Augustine of Canterbury, the apostle of England, and Paulinus the Roman had definite contact with her relatives. Hilda gained friendship with Bishop Aidan of Lindisfarne Island, the second apostle of Northumbria, and he helped her to become established in the monastic life on the River Wear with a few companions. A year later he installed her as abbess at Hartlepool where she served for eight years (647–655). After one of the Oswy clan donated land in fulfillment of a vow after victory in battle, she founded the great double monastery at Whitby, high on the cliffs above the sea.

At Whitby Hilda was the abbess, and ironically it was an abbess who henceforth tended to rule over most Celtic double monasteries in England. Although some claim she used Benedict's rule, she undoubtedly used a combination of many rules. Her original Celtic-rite Bishop Aidan would, no doubt, have given her the customs of Iona, which used the so-called rule of St. Columba. As abbess, she trained both male and female monks in scripture and secular learning, so that many brothers were ordained priests. No less than five were consecrated as bishops as the result of her excellent training.

The layout of the monastery was typically Celtic. A double church actually separated the monks and nuns into two churches within its thick walls. The cells were clustered in the usual Celtic pattern like the semieremitical *skete* or *laura* of the East. Perhaps because of the eremitical dimension, each cell contained two rooms to keep the hermit-monk from "cabin fever." Yet we know that Whitby was a center for much activity despite its semieremitical Celtic pattern. It was a center for evangelization as well as for learning, so that many children of noble birth were sent there for religious and cultural training.

One of the most famous synods in English church history took place at Whitby in the year 663. It was at this synod that the issues and conflicts between Celtic and Roman Christianity would be settled. Hilda, the founder of this now famous Celtic monastery, joined with Bishop Colman of Lindisfarne (Aidan's successor) to champion the Celtic rite. This included a different date for Easter that coincided with John's gospel and the liturgical calendar of Eastern Christianity. Also at issue was the Celtic tonsure, which had its beginnings with the Druids who shaved from the ears forward instead of the typical Roman "bald spot" on top. Also, the more monastic pattern for the entire church was, no doubt, at variance with the more urban, diocesan pattern used by Rome. At this council, Wilfred, a bishop with monastic origins himself, used unusual eloquence to sway the synod of bishops, abbots, and two kings to adherence to the Roman observance. We can only guess that Hilda's Celtic heart was broken when she was forced to renounce the Celtic customs that Bishop Aidan had himself given her at the foundation of her whole monastic life. It was now only a matter of time before the more Roman model would pave the way for enforcing the rule of St. Benedict on all Celtic monasteries, absorbing their unique integrations into the more uniform structures of the Roman church.

Celtic monasticism speaks a particular voice in my heart. God knows that the song of St. Francis forever sings to bring harmony to my soul. Also, I cannot help but feel as close as an intimate brother to St. Antony's hermits of the Eastern desert. The celibate schools of Christian philosophers, as popularized by St. Basil (329–379) and the celibates of St. Jerome's Rome and Bethlehem, call always to the logic of God's holy fire of divine love. Of course, the Celtic monastic tradition of St. Columba and the practical monasticism for the common men of St. Benedict speak deeply to my heart and mind. Likewise, my strong love for the little hermitages of the Marches, which so grace early Franciscan history, as well as the eremitical beginnings of the Observant and Capuchin reforms, call to my innermost heart like a profound and passionate spiritual romance. Further, the hermitages of the Franciscan Brothers and Sisters of Penance (known popularly as the Third Order) seem to knit all these traditions together in the Franciscan expression of the Gregorian reform. In reading these histories, I am struck not only by the particular charism of each founder or foundress, but by the common charism that seems to burn and glow like a mystical fire in and through each founding brother and sister. St. Bonaventure (1217–74), in the wisdom of his last years, calls this universal "order" the holy seraphic, or angelic, order, as contrasted to the organized orders to which he sometimes gave the name "seraphic" also. It is to this universal "order" that I must always belong. I am a Christian "monk" and a monk only. How I wish we had not so confused the meaning of this simple word!

A monk is a person who seeks God alone. A monk is a person on fire with love for God, one who has given up all and separated himself from all in order to know intense mystical union with the Creator of all. A monk should be like a man from another world. The things of this world should be totally tasteless to him. Yet in this holy detachment, the monk should be the person who comes truly to experience the created world with a heightened awareness and heavenly appreciation that comes from knowing the Creator of the world. The monk is the one who turns only to heavenly realms, and so becomes effective on earth. The monk seeks to be a divine creature from another world, and so comes to bring the human reconciliation of Jesus to this world. The monk seeks to be a pilgrim and a stranger, and so is everywhere at home.

Likewise, the monastery should be like a dwelling from another world. The allurements of the secular city should be totally absent in this city of God. Yet the monastery should be a place of true artistic beauty and environmental balance, reflecting as a mirror on the earth the heavenly beauty and balance of the divine Artist. The monastery should be a place of keen environmental beauty and sensitivity, where the delicate and fragile dimensions of all creation are fully experienced, appreciated, and savored, so as to lead the solitary community of monks to constant praise of God. Let the monastery be a place of silence, so that both the small and great dynamic reality of the Living Word of God will always be sensitively received. Let it be a place of environmental asceticism, so as to foster a heightened awareness of the delicate aesthetic beauties of the created world. Yes, let the monastery be like a dwelling from another world, and it will increase sensitivity to the created beauty of all the world and so help lead all creation to God.

I am always struck by both the balanced ascetic rigor and the spiritual flexibility that characterized these founding monks, consecrated to Jesus in solitary and communal lives within their monasteries. All seem to try to discover in their own time the radical call of Jesus to live the gospel of the coming of the Father's kingdom in the desert and in the city, in contemplation and action, in solitude and community. A simple life of following Jesus in gospel poverty and quiet prayer seems to inspire all the first disciples of each founder. They all drew together first in informal communities knit together primarily by the governing power of divine love.

It is only in the second and third generation of each community that rigid governmental forms and particularly popularized charismatic emphasis become necessary for survival. Consequently, we now have hundreds of divided, organized, and often lukewarm communities, who must advertise and champion their founders' heated zeal in order to continue. How I wish we could all burn with that one consuming fire of divine love that unites all founders and foundresses in the universal seraphic "order" dedicated to fulfilling the radical call of Jesus Christ and his holy gospel! This is the true order of Christian monks.

I am eternally grateful to God for the work he has done in the past through the various orders of monks. As a Franciscan, I enjoy great freedom in living out my own call. I just feel God is calling us all to a revolutionary integration of past traditions so as to present something wonderful and new to meet the challenge of the future. That is one of the keys to belonging to this universal order of monks, the order St. Bonaventure called the truly "seraphic order," the order to which every monastic founder and foundress of the past belonged!

In today's world we cannot always see what this spiritual order is or where it is going, for, as life in the Spirit, it is like the wind. We simply know it exists because its mystical reality burns deep within our hearts through the fire of divine love and the powerful wind of the Spirit.

That is why it is so important to understand the lifestyles and spiritualities of those who have burned with this same divine fire in ages past. We can learn from the wisdom they have passed on to us. The wisdom was possessed by both the early Celtic monks and the early Franciscan hermits.

As we now look to the future, we cannot help but be inspired by the Celtic monasticism of Ireland. Deep in the Celtic heritage and tradition of this holy island lies a profound spirituality that calls all Franciscans, all Christians and, yes, all monks, to a life of the radical prayer and poverty of Jesus which cannot help but change the world. It is a call to bring forth revolutionary new communities to meet the challenge of the future. It is from Celtic Ireland that we hear again the gospel of challenge to follow Jesus Christ without compromise. This is also the call of our contemporary Franciscan family. This is the call of the new revolutionary monasticism of the future. This is a call for all Christians everywhere to form the contemplative church of the future.

4

THE CENOBITES

☙

Although this book is primarily about eremitism, it would be wrong to overlook or at least consider the place of the cenobites in monasticism in general. As noted previously, the word "monk" originally meant "alone," or "hermit." The cenobites lived communally. They were a class unto themselves and not really monks. However, as the desert ideal spread West and North, the eremitical and the cenobitical ideals began to merge. Eventually, the use of the words actually reversed—"monk" referring primarily to the cenobitic lifestyle of St. Benedict in the West and St. Basil in the East, and "hermit" referring to those not living in cenobitic "monasteries."

As we have seen, St. Antony is considered the founder of eremitism and therefore of all "monasticism"; St. Pachomius is considered the founder of the cenobites. St. Macarius (c. 300–389) might well be considered the developer of the semi-, or socioeremitical way of life, as he integrated both the seclusion of the anchorite and the community of the cenobites in the classic *skete* or *laura*, where hermit cells are grouped around a common chapel or oratory.

This integration continued with St. John Cassian (c. 400) and St. Basil the Great (d. 379). Cassian was brought up in Syria and Palestine but brought the monastic fire of the Egyptian desert to Gaul, or what we today call France. Cassian definitely favored the cenobitic ideal because he thought it more livable for the average person, but he always left room for the possibility of continuing on into a more anchoritic way of life. His logic went something like this:

The hermit life is the most perfect, but who among us is perfect? Therefore, most of us will do better as cenobites. He also held that the cenobites were first and that the hermits grew out of the cenobitic life, an idea we now know to be not entirely correct. For him the life of the hermit was the full blossoming of desert monasticism, but his moderation and realism caused him to encourage most people to begin monastic life in the cenobium. Thus, he integrates Antony and Pachomius into one community without losing the beauty or uniqueness of either. John Cassian leaves us a rather full description of this life within his *Institutes* and *Conferences*. All later monasticism of the West will consider these almost a "must" for any community rule or book of rules.

St. Basil is considered the father of Eastern monasticism in its present form. He was not nearly so tolerant of hermits and tended to exclude them altogether from his way of life. His reasoning went like this: If the highest law of the gospel is love, and love must be both for God and neighbor, how can the hermit fulfill the gospel toward the neighbor if he or she lives alone? The rule of St. Basil is like all the earlier rules of the monastic East, not so much a legal rule as a description. It does not so much set down legal norms for what will yet be as it simply describes what is.

The rule of St. Basil is the accepted universal rule of Eastern monasticism; however, that monasticism has also deemed it wise to accept the testimony of the eremitical desert fathers. Consequently, eremitism and semieremitism have always found a lasting place in Eastern monasticism alongside the cenobitism of St. Basil.

We should also mention St. Augustine of Hippo (354–430) who developed a definite cenobitical monasticism in Northern Africa. His monastery developed first from the life that he, his mother, and his converted illegitimate son lived together. After the death of both his son and his mother, he developed this life more fully in Africa, where he gathered a group of like-minded brothers around him to help him in his apostolic activity and way of life. He soon became bishop of Hippo but continued to live surrounded by his brother monks. His "rule" is taken from a letter he sent to a group of sisters who lived the communal life inspired by him and his brothers.

St. Augustine's "monastery" was really in no way eremitical. It was a place of communal charity and prayer that served as a base for apostolic and intellectual ministry. His so-called "rule" is a model of sane moderation and upbuilding love that served to stabilize the life of the scholar or apostolic laborer. The communities' use of his so-called "rule" did not continue indefinitely after this original success. It would, however, be taken up by European communities centuries later.

Ironically, this rule would be given to many groups of hermits in Europe during the mendicant era. Thus, its impact is not insignificant in our study of eremitism, and it serves as a constant reminder of the need to make the communal dimension of gospel charity and moderation in some way manifest even within our hermit colonies and our semieremitic communities.

Of course there are the other founders and developers of the monastic ideal in Europe and the Northern Celtic islands. Celtic monasticism is a topic unto itself, for it represents a highly integrated socioeremitism that developed independent of, yet not in opposition to, Rome. The other expressions of European monasticism began to follow a more Roman expression, under the direct influence of "the greats" like Cassian.

The greatest of these "greats" was St. Benedict of Nursia, who wrote his famous rule around 530. What St. Basil's rule is in the East, St. Benedict's rule is in the West. Although Benedict's rule is definitely cenobitic, he recognized the loftiness of the eremitic ideal and made certain provision for those who feel called to the eremitic way of life after having lived for a while as cenobites.

Benedict's rule is not really original, but it is ingenius. In essence he took the existent *Rule of the Master* (written southeast of Rome soon after 500), moderated its excessiveness with the wisdom and traditional rootedness of Cassian, and came up with a very sane and balanced monastic rule for his own small community south of Rome at Monte Cassino. In this he integrated both the eremitic and the cenobitic life into a moderate monasticism that makes a proper place for all. The idea of a "Benedictine Order," or a group of monasteries united under one rule, and most especially under one general superior, was an alien concept to St. Benedict and the monks of Europe for many centuries after his death. In this they followed very much the pattern of Eastern monasticism and what still remains the pattern in the East today.

Things continued in this fashion until the coronation of Charlemagne as emperor of Rome on Christmas Day in the year A.D. 800. Charlemagne had a love for monasticism and did all that he could to help it prosper throughout the Empire. Likewise, his successor, Louis the Pious, had a similar love and vision. However, Louis decided that if the monastic life was to succeed, a major reform and reorganization was needed.

It was then that Louis appointed the "second" St. Benedict, Benedict of Aniane, to reform all of monastic Europe under the *Rule of St. Benedict*. The plan was simple: Put all monasteries within the reach of Benedict of Aniane under the Benedictine rule and give Benedict of Aniane power as the emperor's representative to ensure that the reform was carried out. All abuses would be cleared up by a neat and uniform adherence to the *Rule of St. Benedict*.

In reality the effects of this grand reform were extremely limited. The more pluriform and eclectic monastic tradition would not easily give way to superficial adherance to only one rule, even if enforced from the top by the emperor through Benedict of Aniane. Needless to say, this grand reform lost almost all momentum upon Benedict's death in A.D. 821. But a major change had taken place: The emperor of Roman Christendom had publicly recognized only one form of monasticism for all monastic Europe—Benedictine monasticism.

The next major change came in the tenth and eleventh centuries with the Cluniac reform. The use of the *Rule of St. Benedict* became mandatory along with rather extensive legislation on how the rule was lived at Cluny. Especially under the abbots St. Odilo (994–1049) and St. Hugh (1049–1109) many monasteries adopted these additional "usages." Furthermore, Cluny began to found daughter houses, or priories, that used the customs of Cluny even after they came independent abbeys under their own abbot. During the heyday of Cluny, however, even these abbeys were dependent on the legislation *and* the leadership of Cluny. Thus, even the monks of these other monasteries professed vows that were received not by their own abbot but by the abbot of Cluny.

The long tradition of universal monasticism had gone around a major corner in its development. Instead of having independent monasteries that draw upon the collective wisdom of all monasticism, the Cluniac reform created a group of individuals living in various communities under one common superior and professing one common rule and constitution. This was novel. It was new. It built from the monastic tradition, but also broke from an age-old tradition of independence and eclectic approaches to rules and legislation.

The actual content of their lifestyle is also important. In the beginning monastic life was simple and austere. The monks lived from the work of their own hands. Their liturgy was simple and unadorned, leaving ample time for private prayer and manual labor. The monasteries were small, comprised of twenty or so poor men who gave themselves completely to God. All this changed when the monasteries became estates of both monks and secular serfs over which the abbots and officers of the monastery ruled like lords. The liturgy became more and more elaborate until almost all of the monk's day was spent in choir. Apart from choir, the monk was apt to engage either in scholastic study or in the administration of one of the many activities of the monastery, usually finding professional laborers and artists from among the laity. The life lived even by St. Benedict and his first monks was barely to be found among his overgrown child called "Benedictinism."

It was from this environment that the eleventh-century reformers sprang. Romuald, Bruno, Peter Damian, and others burst forth with an eremitical explosion that rekindled the original fire of the desert fathers throughout monastic Europe. Owing to the religious climate of the day they might well have kept the now universal *Rule of St. Benedict,* but they broke loose entirely from the usages and customs of Cluny that had so dominated the monastic world of the West.

It is important for us here to obtain a picture of how limited the Cluniac and the traditional Benedictine hold was on the more universal approach to monasticism. Cluny ruled for about one hundred and fifty years. Some of those years were building years, with no real legal authority prevailing over other monasteries. Some of those years were years of legal power, but with no real zeal or inspiration. So it was toward the end. Not even one hundred years were really quality years of both legal and spiritual power. As soon as the zeal to live the pristine and primitive life of the first monks was cooled and squelched, it was only a matter of time before God would raise it up again, this time outside of the seemingly god-like kingdom of Cluny.

Keeping in mind the limited success of Benedict of Aniane, coupled with a more real view of the "rule" of Cluny, we begin to see how brief was the seemingly universal reign of Benedictine monasticism. From the third and fourth centuries until the ninth century, a pluriform tradition of independent monasteries drawing from many rules was the norm. The tenth century alone saw a universal, uniform adherence to one particular expression of Benedictinism. This, too, was a low point in monastic history. By the eleventh century we see an explosion of reforms bringing back a more pluriform expression of monasticism from the Eastern deserts of the Christian past into the mountains and hills of the Christian West.

Needless to say, eremitism was always a part of this more universal approach to monasticism. Integrating a viable cenobitism with an authentic eremitism, the earlier forms of European monasticism and the eleventh-century reformers allowed for a socioeremitism that could really be called "monastic," in a tradition that created a communal environment for a man or woman to encounter God "alone."

It should also be remembered with thanks that the Cluniac reform allowed for anchorites to be attached to monasteries. In some cases these hermits had to "secularize," or be dispensed from their vows, but at least some provision for this way of life was made. Furthermore, it should be remembered that reformers such as St. Romuald began their monastic life within the Cluniac "system," as did the Cistercians, who began their reform with Stephen Harding under the "endorsement" of Molesme, a famous abbey of the Cluniac observance.

In all fairness to Cluny, it should be remembered that most all eleventh-century reforms came forth from her. It was only when fiery young reformers leveled attacks on Cluny's lifestyle that Cluny sought an answer from her own tradition. This unfortunately led to rivalries, the most famous being between the Cistercian abbot and reformer St. Bernard of Clairvaux (1090–1153) and Peter the Venerable, abbot of Cluny from 1122–56. Furthermore, most of these eleventh-century reforms kept some of Cluny's novel developments, such as the order-like centralization that paved the way for the bona fide religious orders founded by the mendicants such as St. Francis of Assisi.

Also, all of Western civilization owes a great debt to the great Benedictine abbeys such as Cluny for their great contribution to scholastic and artistic endeavors. These abbeys literally kept civilization alive during the so-called "Dark Ages" and contributed much to the scholarly, artistic, and scientific furtherance of the whole human race which would blossom in the mendicant era under the great Franciscan and Dominican scholars and saints.

From all this we can see a great debt owed by Franciscan eremitism even to the cenobites. The Franciscan hermitage always remains a place of brotherhood and community. It is semi- or socioeremitic. In this it owes a great debt to the pluriform expressions of early monastic Europe, as well as to the wide array of eleventh-century semieremitical and contemplative reformers. In light of the centralized nature of Francis's gospel brotherhood, we ever owe much to the organization of the Cluniac reform. The scholarly tradition of the Benedictine monks did much to pave the way for the Franciscan scholars, who themselves were often hermits. Furthermore, the gift of the Portiuncula from the Benedictines to the Franciscans stands as a symbol and places the Franciscans in perpetual debt to the cenobitic Benedictines.

5

THE GREGORIAN REFORM

Of all the religious movements that influenced Francis of Assisi, it was the Gregorian reform that most directly shaped the environment which served as the womb for the entire Franciscan family. As a reaction to the laxity among both clergy and laity, the Gregorian reform called for a radical return to the simple Christian life which followed the gospel of Jesus Christ without compromise. This reformed lifestyle affected existing monastic communities, and gave birth to many new forms of Christian community that attempted to return to the purity of the gospels and the fathers of the early church within the contemporary situation of the early second millenneum. This reform touched the movement, or class, within the church called "the Penitents." This class, or order, included both married and celibate brothers and sisters, thus giving rise to many new lay communities resembling the community described in the second chapter of Acts in Jerusalem, or the covenant communities of today's church. Even more importantly, the Gregorian reform called for a return to the extreme gospel poverty and contemplative prayer that was so radically and successfully exemplified by the informal eremitical life of the desert fathers. Thus, many new monastic or semimonastic communities developed during the Gregorian reform which were forerunners of the simple Franciscan life of gospel poverty and prayer as it was lived in the little mountain hermitages of Italy.

The main eremitical, monastic communities that influenced Francis of Assisi were the Camaldolese, the Carthusians, the monks of Fonte Avella, and the Grandmontersians. Each of these communities attempted to bring the original purity of the gospels and the desert fathers into the world in which they lived. This meant that a mere mimicking of past communities would not do. They had to live the primitive gospel life that allowed for similar integrations of the early hermits of the desert, yet in developed ways that were creative and new. These new communities each developed its own particular way of creative integration that was beautifully unique and true to the gospel. A short study of their various attempts to live the gospel of Jesus without compromise can shed even further light on both the uniqueness and the historical and traditional rootedness of Francis of Assisi's lifestyle within the Franciscan hermitage.

The Camaldolese Hermits: St. Romuald

The Camaldolese hermits, founded by St. Romuald (c. 952–1027), had one of the most strikingly similar lifestyles to the approach of the Franciscan hermitage. The similarities between the Franciscan and Camaldolese hermits are so profound that they require a separate study which we can only summarize here. However, there are some general observations that can be fairly made without injustices.

The Camaldolese and the Franciscan hermitages both represent very pure Western developments of the eremitical colonies of the Eastern desert tradition. The Camaldolese, more than any other Gregorian Franciscan forerunner, manifest the most direct structural and charismatic influence from the semieremitic *skete* of the East. A small colony of isolated or physically separated huts, or cells, centered around a chapel, formed the Camaldolese "hermitage." Like the desert fathers' *skete*, this manifested a working integration between strict seclusion and healthy community relationships. The whole community gathered only once weekly in the church for a eucharistic liturgy. The daily chanting of the psalms in common in the church was the responsibility of only a few of the hermits, leaving the majority of the hermits to chant the office in the solitude of their cells. Meals were taken in the hermit's cell alone, and silence perpetually kept; however, silence was not absolute nor were common meals totally neglected. The poverty of Camaldoli food, clothing, and shelter was extreme, yet common ownership was moderately practiced. All of this greatly resembles the life of the less formal Franciscan hermitage.

The main innovation of the Camaldolese was the establishment of a cenobitic sister monastery to serve as a hospice for pilgrims, a refuge for sick or elderly hermits, and a training community for prospective hermits. It was the job of the active cenobitic monastery to meet the physical needs of the contemplative hermits, yet the hermits retained governmental control to insure the eremitical integrity of the entire contemplative foundation. The establishment of a separate class of monks called "lay brothers" to staff this active monastery further helped to guarantee the undisturbed solitude and silence of the strict hermit-monk. This also gave a place in the life of the community to those who might be called to a life of prayer, but who were not called to the strict solitude and intensity of life lived by the hermits themselves. Therefore, a real working flexibility is manifested in this bilevel integration that opened the community to the cenobitic many in the love of Christ, yet retained the integrity of the eremitical few in God's wisdom. Though Francis fought against the abuse of this "choir-monk" and "lay-brother" class system in his day, he did seek the same flexibility in his hermitages.

A further similarity with the Franciscan ideal can be seen in the apostolic zeal and activity of Romuald himself. Like Francis, Romuald spent most of his life in the solitude of the hermitage, but also like Francis, Romuald traveled throughout Italy preaching repentance and reform. Thus, Romuald was personally responsible for the reform of over one hundred monasteries, inspiring many of these to persevere in returning to the desert ideal from which they came. Francis himself founded over twenty such hermitages.

Unlike Francis, Romuald never totally broke with the Benedictine rule which was so strong in the West. A real "sobriety" pervades the Camaldolese spirit of joy, not quite as externally free as the spirit of Franciscan joy. However, Romuald's own interpretation of that Benedictine rule comes surprisingly close to the Franciscan ideal of joy in many ways. Likewise, Romuald never seemed to touch the average Christian as effectively as Francis did, and his reform was primarily in monastic communities. Francis's preaching and example sparked a fire of the Spirit that literally swept through every level of Christian life in the West, and eventually throughout the entire world. The similarities between Francis and Romuald far outnumber the differences.

Fonte Avella: St. Peter Damian (1007–72)

Probably the most popular pre-Franciscan Gregorian reformer was St. Peter Damian, a hermit-preacher from the monastic hermitage of Fonte Avella. It was Peter Damian who had the most influence on the married and celibate penitents who would later affiliate with Francis as "Brothers and Sisters of Penance." It was Peter Damian who foreshadowed Francis in popularizing devotion to the passion of Jesus, a penitential lifestyle for all Christians, and devotion to Mary, mother of Jesus our God. He also inspired a monastic reform of the hermit life of extreme poverty and prayer through his preaching, his writing, and his lifestyle. Peter Damian and the life of the hermits of Fonte Avella were an important influence on the religious environment that shaped the eremitical lifestyle of Francis and the first Franciscan hermits.

Actually, Peter Damian joined Fonte Avella; he did not found it. It consisted of a simple group of independent hermits who followed the *Rule of St. Benedict* in eremitical zeal and fervor. With a great background in both holiness and literary talent, Peter Damian soon was made superior of the monastery, thus making Fonte Avella a model for eremitical life in spirituality and structure. In his success, he was to be made cardinal archbishop of Ostia by Pope Stephen IX in A.D. 1057. Peter virtuously retained his monastic discipline even while in office, but was allowed to retire again to the hermit life he loved with Pope Alexander II's full approval in 1067. He died in 1073, a holy hermit-monk of Fonte Avella.

Peter Damian followed the structure of St. Romuald's Camaldolese, establishing a cenobitic monastery of *conversi*, or "lay brothers," who took care of the hermitage of hermit-monks. However, unlike the later Camaldolese, the only binding "rule" between the cenobitic and the eremitic communities was the "law" of charity. They existed as two independent institutions in all legal and governmental matters. Yet we see that the novices of the hermitage lived for awhile in the cenobitic monastery before they were deemed worthy to live a life of solitude, thus testing their vocation in the *cenobium* before allowing them to advance to the hermitage. An integration between solitude and community existed on this level.

Like the Camaldolese, the hermits of Fonte Avella met only once a week on Sunday for Mass and a chapter of faults. In the privacy of their cells they said all the canonical prayer hours, plus an extreme number of mandatory, additional prayers, exceeding even the number advised by Romuald. The poverty and penance of Fonte Avella were similar to Camaldoli, yet seem to be more extreme.

In light of these similarities with the Camaldoli, it is not surprising to find that Fonte Avella was officially attached to the Order of Camaldoli in 1570. In fact, there are those who feel that Peter Damian's Fonte Avella considered itself "Camaldolese" from the very beginning, owing to its self-confessed heavy reliance on Camaldolese usages and the fact that Peter Damian was Romuald's first principal biographer. The more extreme poverty and penances of Fonte Avella gives us a clearer picture of the actual usages of the Camaldolese under Romuald before the later constitution of Blessed Rudolf was adopted, which greatly modified some of the more intense and earlier customs of Romuald.

All of this has direct relevance to early Franciscan history. It seems that Cardinal Ugolino (c. 1170–1241), the cardinal protector of the Franciscan Order and the close friend and advisor of Francis, is considered by some to have been a Camaldolese abbot. As cardinal protector, Ugolino was actively involved in the spiritual and legal formation of the so-called First, Second, and Third Orders of St. Francis. Thus, it is not surprising to find Francis and Ugolino traditionally making thirty-day retreats together at the hermitages of Camaldoli to work out internal problems within the First Order, and to plot a course for the legal establishment of the "Brothers and Sisters of Penance" as a legitimate religious order of their own. Furthermore, contrary to the earlier belief that Ugolino gave Cistercian constitutions to Clare, it seems that Ugolino actually gave the Poor Ladies the constitutions of Fonte Avella as their first rule, thus linking the contemplative sisters of St. Clare very early to the earliest Camaldolese tradition, both in the person of Cardinal Ugolino and in law.

Other studies also link many Franciscan hermitages with the Camaldolese traditions. It seems that many of the first Franciscan "places" could have been gifts from the Camaldolese. One of these, Monte Casela, became a hermitage for Franciscan penitents, then later passed into the authority of the Capuchins who, by the way, were aided greatly by the Camaldolese in their early years. Most surprising is the Portiuncula itself, the cradle of the Franciscan Order. Some believe that the "Benedictines" who gave this place to Francis were actually Camaldolese monks. So it is not at all surprising to see the life of Francis and the first brothers in this holy place greatly resembling the hermit life of the Camaldolese and the desert fathers' *sketes.*

All in all, both Camaldoli and Fonte Avella show great resemblances to what later come to be known as the Franciscan hermitage. The emphasis on Spirit-filled solitude, silence, poverty, and penance in the midst of the semieremitical community life of a family resembling the desert fathers' *skete* is evident in them all. Also a further integration between contemplation and action is seen in Romuald, Peter Damian, and Francis.

While Peter Damian especially seems to have popularized a life of conversion among the married and celibate "pentitents," both Romuald and Peter Damian were still concerned primarily with a reform of traditional Benedictine monasticism. It was Francis alone who was able to reform the early monastic ideals, while breaking boldly into a revolutionary new dimension of community that spanned across all classes of Christians, and constituted the establishment of a whole new rule in the church.

Carthusians: St. Bruno of Cologne (925–965)

The eremitical community of the Gregorian reform that has most successfully survived the changing religious climates of the passing years is the Carthusian Order, founded by St. Bruno of Cologne. The fact that his community has never needed internal reform indicates quite a lot about the seriousness of the men who entered this life and the pure workability of their rule. They are often considered the crowning glory of Western eremitism.

Bruno himself was a scholar who, after being disillusioned by what he saw of the clergy during his past as chancellor of his archdiocese, retired with two companions to a mountain hermitage belonging to the monks of Molesme. They lived their life of prayer under the protection of Abbot Robert (c. 1027–1110), yet did not seem actually to become vowed monks of Molesme. Finding this holy cenobitic place still inadequate for the pure hermit life, they retired deep into the wilderness and began a regular eremitical life in 1084. In 1090, after six years of work, prayer, and peace, Bruno's old student, Pope Urban II, summoned Bruno to Rome to help him in council. At this, the small community of hermits dispersed, but Bruno sent his disciples back to the hermitage to continue the life without him. Bruno would never be given papal permission to return to his beloved Grand Charterhouse. Finally, toward the end of Bruno's life, the pope gave him permission to found a new Carthusian charterhouse in Calabria, Italy. After this Bruno died.

With this brief overview of Bruno's life, we can see a great difference from the eremitical life of Francis. Bruno was a scholar who seemed to be involved in the scholarly life of the church all his life. Francis was an average layman, innocently accepting of good scholars, yet never seeking scholarship for himself or his brothers. Bruno was much influenced by the monastic order of Molesme in the structuring of his hermitage. Francis's hermitages were informal, family-like affairs where an intense life of prayer was guided more by the wind of the Spirit than by a solid external structure. Yet, both Bruno and Francis tried to live a life of gospel poverty and prayer in reaction to the abuses and laxity that seemed so common in the church of their day.

Like the Camaldolese or the Franciscan hermitage, the Carthusian charterhouse sought to bring the semieremitical life of the Eastern desert to the eleventh-century church of the West. Unlike the Franciscan hermitage, however, the Carthusian charterhouse was still very much a formal monastery. Like the hermits of the Eastern *skete*, the charterhouse was made up of a central chapel with individual hermit cells around it. These cells were all attached and connected to one another by a large enclosed cloister, or passageway. The "cell" itself consisted of a rather large four-room apartment with two workrooms downstairs and two rooms upstairs for prayer, study, and daily living. A good-sized private garden was attached to each cell. In this the physical layout of the Western cenobitic monastery cloister was still very much evident and regular monastic moderation retained.

However, the Carthusian life was still very much an intense hermit's life. The Carthusian hermit spent almost all his time within the silence of his cell. For this reason the cells and gardens were quite large. The hermit would venture into the church only three times a day for Matins, Vespers, and a two- or three-hour vigil every night. Mass would be celebrated in common only on Sundays or on special feasts. All other formal and informal prayers would be prayed in the cell. All work was done either in the cell's workroom or in the cell's garden. Daily meals would be taken in the cell except one common meal a week in the refectory. Of course, this strict solitude naturally enforced a strict and nearly continual silence, which was broken only once a week during a chapter of faults and a community recreation walk outside the charterhouse. In this intense solitude and silence, only a true contemplative hermit could survive.

The charterhouse also had the classes of lay brothers, *conversi*, and domestics to share and aid in the life of the monastery according to each one's capacity. In this the life of community was even further integrated into the semieremitic life of the charterhouse. Also, since these brothers were responsible for most of the upkeep of the monastery and the income-producing work, the contemplative environment was structurally guaranteed for the hermit choir monks. The lay brother was a fully vowed member of a more cenobitic community that was directly attached to the church and choir monks' cloister. The brother's life involved more community interaction during work on the monastery, but still required a high degree of contemplative silence. The habited *conversi* brother did not take formal vows, but took informal promises like vows, and thus entered into much of the lay-brother community life. He was responsible for much of the business dealings with those from outside the charterhouse, and thus was given more freedom from strict silence. The domestic was a nonhabited member of the community who also made informal promises. The domestic was given much freedom from the monastic schedule, but did much to take care of the external needs of the monastery. In all this a happy plurality of community expressions was structurally provided for, thus allowing many different types of men to respond to God's call to a life of prayer within the Carthusian community. This integration between solitude and community was a workable and commendable application of the desert-father ideal.

However, the strict separation between the cleric choir-monk hermit and the lay-brother community worker does pose some historical problems. It seems that when one entered the charterhouse, he either joined the choir-monk community and became both a priest and a full-time hermit, or he joined the lay-brother community. The novice classes were totally separate, and crossing from one community to the other after monastic profession was impossible without going through a new novitiate in the other respective community. Thus the pure desert-father ideal of a Spirit-led rhythm between and graduation from the *cenobium* to the *skete* was structurally almost impossible. In addition, a subtle clericalism was strongly supported in the Carthusian system, which put them on an opposite end of the spectrum from the strongly lay character of the pure desert-father ideal.

Even with some of the historical problems this highly organized Western expression of monastic eremitism poses in reference to the early *skete* of the Eastern desert it was trying to copy, it is still true that the Carthusian charterhouse is one of the more important expressions of the hermit life within all of Christian history. An intense life of poverty and prayer was lived in a way that left freedom for various types of men within the Charterhouse. A working integration between solitude and communion was seen on many levels, thus applying the similar integrations of the desert fathers in a developed manner within the institutional world in which the Carthusian lived. In all this they were very similar to the flexible life of the Franciscan hermitage, where both active "mothers" and contemplative "sons" lived together in peaceful harmony. In this the Carthusian charterhouse and the Franciscan hermitage join as brothers and become one.

Grandmontersians: St. Stephen of Muret (c. 1045–1124)

Probably one of the more radical communities among the eremitical forerunners of Francis was St. Stephen of Muret and his order of Grandmontersians. This community patterned itself after the regular observances of the Camaldolese and the Carthusians, yet the Grandmontersians broke out of most all Western monastic forms in their attempt simply to follow the gospel. In this they have much in common with Francis.

Stephen was a student in Rome who felt a deeper call to solitude, based on his knowledge of Greek anchorite practices. After living for one year in solitary seclusion, he attracted disciples and built a "monastery." The interesting thing about this informal prayer community is that they followed no written rule beyond the gospel, and considered themselves neither canons, nor monks, nor hermits. Likewise, Stephen considered himself neither an abbot nor a prior, but simply a lay "corrector," much resembling the elders of today's lay covenant communities.

Yet Stephen still outlined some forms for organization. He spoke of the members' "profession" into the community and adopted a penitential garb as the habit for the professed members of the community. Later the *Rule of St. Stephen* was compiled by the fourth "corrector," by then called a "prior," which contained the customs of St. Stephen, excerpts of the Benedictine rule, and the customs of the Carthusians.

From this "way of life" some definite organization is evident. It seems that like the Carthusians, the hermits were to be clerics who were devoted totally to solitary prayer. A community of *conversi* brothers took care of the material needs of the hermits. Beyond this, an extreme life of penance was expected of all.

The most unusual aspects of this community are to be found in its extreme application and guarding of solitude, silence, and poverty. It seems that in order to guard the full solitude and silence of the cleric-hermits, the *conversi* brothers were responsible for all external concerns of the monastery, including its administration.

The *conversi* were considered hermits in that the entire foundation was to be "a community of solitaries." Because of this, no lay people were allowed to attend their common prayer or eucharistic liturgies. Absolutely no preaching apostolate was allowed on or off the monastery grounds, either by the clerics or the *conversi*. Furthermore, even the *conversi* brothers were forbidden to have business contacts with either the church or the world, thus limiting their work to the foresting of their own land. A life of extreme poverty guaranteed a limitation to their active business affairs and further guarded the contemplative life of the *conversi* brothers.

Even with all these extremes, the Grandmontersians had much in common with the Franciscans. They were one of the early Gregorian communities substantially to break from the Benedictine rule in order to use the gospel as their only rule, and still gain papal approval. Their use of the *conversi* brothers and cleric hermits, along with most other Gregorian contemplative communities, foreshadow Francis's use of the active "mother" and the contemplative "son" in his hermitages. Absolute poverty and solitude was a statement against the monastic feudal system, where rich monks were the lords over huge estates worked by poor lay people with families. Francis's poverty had the same purpose.

Finally, in considering themselves neither canons, monks, nor hermits, the Grandmontersians paved the way for Francis to return to the simple status-less state of those first Eastern solitaries who simply sought to follow the gospel of Jesus Christ.

6

THE PENITENTIAL
MOVEMENT

⁂

One of the most important informal, spiritual movements to influence Francis's simple and flexible approach to eremitism was the penitential movement. Ironically, this movement began long before the substantially monastic Gregorian reform as a nonmonastic lay movement, yet was one of the more powerful and far-reaching communal entities of that reform. This movement actually began long before in the early church as the canonical state of public penance for persons who had committed grave, publicly recognized sins. However, as the normal Christian community became more spiritually and morally lax after the time of Constantine, many serious and virtuous Christians willingly entered into this order of penitents in order radically to live a humbler, more self-sacrificing gospel life with the full approval and support of the church. Soon the order of penitents developed into a strong lay movement that included persons or communities that were interested in radically living the gospel of Jesus Christ without compromise.

One of these types was the solitary hermit and the hermit colonies that sprang up from God within the penitential movement. As both individuals and communities, this eremitical dimension of the penitential state had a very great impact on what would soon be called the Franciscan hermitage.

One of the greatest aspects of this movement was its strongly lay character. In reaction to the widespread abuses seen in much of the monastic life and the clerical state, many people sought to live the hermit life within the penitential "state." The hermit-penitents then formally passed from the secular order to the order of penitents without having to compromise their ideals by entering into either the monastic order or the clerical order to gain the proper approval of the church for their particular way of life. Entrance into the penitential state was a formal ecclesiastical act involving the full approval of a bishop, a change of external garb to a penitent's habit, and a commitment to a radically changed lifestyle. Eremitical colonies often required an informal commitment of the three evangelical counsels of obedience, chastity, and poverty in a way similar to the commitment of the first hermits of the Eastern deserts. In this the hermit colonies were a radically authentic attempt to return to the informal vows of the desert fathers from which nearly all formal religious orders sprang. As such, these penitent-hermits were no longer seculars nor were they vowed monks, but they constituted an informally religious, eremitical expression within a distinct order in the church that was both authentic and unique. Yet, like the first hermits of the desert, these hermits were still lay people.

It was the lay character of the penitent-hermits that gave this order an authentic similarity with the earliest desert-father tradition of eremitism. Like the desert fathers, the penitents who made up the hermit colonies were not formally vowed monks in the legally developed, Western understanding of the word. Nor were many of these penitent-hermits deacons or priests. Like the desert fathers before them, the hermits of the penitential movement sought to live the radical and uncompromising gospel in totally committed simplicity, yet without the privileges and notoriety, or the abuses, of the monastic or clerical states.

One of the notable aspects of the penitential movement that gave an even more authentic freedom to their hermits was the concept and practice of being a "prilgrim." It was a common custom among the penitents of the Gregorian reform to make a pilgrimage on foot to the Holy Land. This pilgrimage usually took the remainder of one's life. The idea behind this was to spend one's life wandering in absolute poverty in the very land where Jesus himself wandered as a poor, itinerant preacher giving his life for the life of the world. This sense of pilgrimage gave even the solitary hermits a pilgrim's mobility which allowed them to go beyond the Western concept of strict cloister, and return to a more flexible concept of the solitary life that more authentically represented the desert tradition.

The penitential practice of being a pilgrim soon gave rise to the vocation of the itinerant preacher. These preachers were, again, laymen who sought to call the church to simple but profound reform through the example of an extremely radical lifestyle and words of admonition that received power from their own life experience. Like the pilgrim, this penitential vocation was a strong witness for a return to both the poverty and the simple flexibility of Jesus, as these lay preachers wandered with the holy wind of the Spirit to proclaim the fullness of the Father's kingdom.

The pilgrim-like vocation of the itinerant preacher also added yet another authenticating flexibility to the eremitical expressions of the order of penitents. Following the primary example of Jesus and the secondary example of the desert fathers, the hermits of the penitential movement soon began not only to wander as pilgrims, but also to take up the vocation of preaching the gospel message of penance for the remission of sins of all the world. Their words and their lifestyle were simple, yet the impact of both had an effect on people that was nothing less than profound. Thus, the penitent hermit-preachers became a very authentic representation of the flexible, yet extremely rigorous and uncompromising, Spirit-led tradition that dates back to the earliest desert fathers and the life of Christ himself.

Since the penitential movement as a whole touched a wide variety of lay-community expressions, the penitent-hermits within the movement often tended to be very open to various communal expressions associating with their strict eremitical colonies. Consequently, we find very strict hermitage communities of celibates existing as a core group reaching out to a larger contemplative community of penitents existing as a satellite group. This satellite group could include more free emphasis on the active life and a membership that might involve both celibates and even married couples. Thus, some of these contemplative communities entered into a radical gospel life that could be seen as nothing short of revolutionary both for Francis's day and for ours.

These penitent hermit colonies enjoyed freedom from an obligation to sing the divine office in monastic choir, thus allowing them to experiment liberally with common prayer. Their so-called ignorance provided a unique opportunity to give witness to the "foolishness" of gospel wisdom, which is found in cultivating the simple prayer of the heart. The use of spontaneous prayer and mantra-like repetitive devotions such as the Jesus prayer and the rosary often formed the main structure of their common prayer. Very few lay people could read, thus making the use of a psalter or a Bible almost impossible. Likewise, freedom from the obligation of the daily monastic office allowed their preachers an even further freedom to wander in the itinerancy of the ministry of Jesus. This, too, said much to Francis—and still says much to us today.

However, plurality and flexibility became both the strength and the weakness of the eremitical expressions of the penitential movement. Because the penitential contemplative communities were not formally vowed, they often lacked the stability that a serious, binding commitment maintained; so eventual acceptance of public, religious vows became an aid and a further witness of the church's formal support and protection. By moving into religious vows, however, these communities were often moved into a more Western legal sense of monasticism. With the formal vows of Western monasticism, they often lost the informal flexibility that made them such an easy instrument for the wind of the Spirit in their earlier years. Also, their spontaneity and simplicity in public prayer soon gave way to various abuses and simplistic repetition, making the formal monastic use of the divine office a more necessary development. The beautiful freedom of the itinerant hermit-preacher was soon sullied by many well-meaning preachers who entered headlong into heretical teachings, thus prompting the church to enforce strongly its law that only clerics could preach to the people regarding "deeper" theological topics, such as church structure and sacraments. This was another major cause for the communities not only to seek the support of the church as vowed religious, but also to actively seek the clerical offices of deacon and priest in order to preach properly and freely the gospel message that burned in their hearts.

Finally, the pluralization of community goals and membership between celibates and family members caused many legitimate hermit colonies eventually to "degenerate" from their original purpose into substantially active, apostolic communities, or even further, into simple secular fraternities.

Even with these admitted weaknesses, the eremitical dimension of the penitential movement said much to Francis of Assisi and still has much to say to us today. The informal simplicity of their lifestyle made them flexible tools for the spontaneous work of the Spirit, who himself calls the world to repentance and raises up an alternative Christian community where charitable love is the greatest law.

The uncompromising and rigorous search for the gospel purity of poverty and prayer caused these hermits to become a respected, popular, and effective spiritual force of renewal and reform within the tenth- to twelfth-century world. It is not at all surprising that before Francis gained a full direction from God regarding his vocation, we find him dressed as a hermit within the order of penitents.

7

THE MENDICANTS

With the surfacing of the itinerant hermit-preacher of the penitential movement, it was only a matter of time before entire orders or communities of this way of life were developed within the church. The Dominicans, Augustinians, Carmelites, and the Franciscans were all a part of this movement of the new style of community. Francis himself began as an individual penitent, with his Order of Friars Minor growing from the base of the life Francis discovered as a solitary member of the order of penance.

The mendicants differed greatly from their monastic predecessors. Instead of patterning their community on the stable, self-supporting, pattern of Acts 2, they took as their model the apostolic and itinerant life of Matthew 10. The monks and hermits of the past stayed in one place, working with their hands or other skills and talents as an example of stability. The mendicant friars, or brothers, wandered from place to place preaching the gospel and living from day to day off the hospitality and generosity of those to whom they ministered. The monks and hermits developed tangible trades. The mendicants preached. It was from this they were given the title "mendicant," open-handed, or "beggar."

Yet, even as mendicants, the eremitical life was still of primary importance. Patterning their life entirely on the gospels, they could not help but notice the large amount of time Jesus spent in solitude. They did not seek to establish their own hermitages or develop monastic villages or centers, but they did place strong emphasis on the importance of some kind of hermitage for solitary prayer. While in the beginning this might have taken the form of impromptu places of retreat, such as abandoned caves, sheds, or churches, they soon established more fixed hermitages on the outskirts of the villages and cities in which they ministered.

With this the hermitages of the mendicants took much from the eremitical patterns of the past. Though the friars did not own their hermitages, or vast acres of land and houses around them, they did follow the classic *skete* or *laura* pattern in laying them out. In emphasizing apostolic poverty, this usually amounted to only a few caves or huts scattered around a common area for prayer and eating. Sometimes this would be adapted to city life where each brother was insured at least the privacy of his own cell within a common house, a privacy unheard of in religious life of that time.

We can thus see that although the mendicants of the twelfth, thirteenth, and fourteenth centuries differed greatly from their monastic predecessors, they still shared much in common with the overall eremitical tradition. Let us now look at some of the mendicant hermits.

The Carmelites

Like the Franciscans, the Carmelites were part of the thirteenth-century mendicant movement of the West. Also, like the Franciscans, they had strong eremitical origins.

It seems that during the Crusades, pilgrims flocked to the Holy Land. After fulfilling their vow of pilgrimage, many took up the hermit life at a particular holy place. These places became centers for loose-knit eremitical colonies. Such places included the mountains and desert of temptation around Jericho, the Mount of Transfiguration toward Galilee, and the range of Mt. Carmal by the Mediterranean Sea. After the victory of Saladin at Hattin in 1187, the only area left to the Christians was Acre and some areas along the Mediterranean coast. Thus, Mt. Carmel became the only remaining eremitical colony in the Holy Land. It was during this period that the formal beginnings of the Carmelites is to be found.

After years of living as an informal colony of hermits, the Carmelites decided they wanted a more formal organization. One of their members, Brocard, began exercising a sort of leadership role among them. In time they approached the papal legate and patriach of Jerusalem, Albert of Vercelli (1149–1214), who resided at Acre, to set down a formal way of life for them. Sometime between 1200 and 1214, he wrote a rule for the hermits of Mt. Carmel.

This rule stands as the only purely eremitical rule in the Christian West and is thus highly important. All other eremitical communities came to profess an existing rule, and then follow their own eremitical constitutions or statutes. Only the hermits of Mt. Carmel obtained their own eremitical rule as something intentional and unique in the church. This cannot be overemphasized.

From this rule and other sources we can learn much about their life, for the rule sought not to set down a new life, but to describe, formalize, and approve the lives they were already living. We know they lived according to the classical *laura* or *skete* pattern of the desert fathers of the East. Each hermit had his own cell apart from the rest, yet there was a common oratory or church in which they came together for daily Mass. It is not clear whether they prayed the divine office in common. However, they did pray the hours and meditated on the scriptures daily in private. Jacques Devitry (c. 1170–1240), bishop of Acre and commentator on many religious communities of his time, says of them: "Others in imitation of the holy anchorite and prophet Elijah, led solitary lives on Mt. Carmel ... where in little comb-like cells, those bees of the Lord laid up sweet spiritual honey."

The hermits' connection to the tradition of the prophet Elijah is not at all insignificant. Mt. Carmel had been connected to the prophet Elijah by all pilgrims with whom he sojourned there during his life. The recognized father of monasticism and eremitism, St. Antony, viewed the prophet Elijah as the model for all Christian ascetics. Jerome contrasts the apostolic model of the bishops and priests of the church with the prophetic model of hermits and monks: "We, however, have proposed for emulation our Pauls, Anthonys, Julians, Maconos, and—if I may have recourse to the authority of Holy Writ—our leader Elijah, or Elisha, our sons of the prophets who dwell in the fields and solitary places and pitched their tents by the waters of the Jordon."

Perhaps with this in mind the Carmelites adopted a habit of rough, undyed wool, consisting of a tunic, a scapular, and a hood. As a cincture they used a leather belt in imitation of Elijah and John the Baptist. They also wore a distinctive mantle of white with brown stripes. This is seen frequently in Middle Age paintings of hermits in the desert.

The hermits on Mt. Carmel received papal confirmation of their eremitical rule in 1226, the year of St. Francis's death. The Fourth

Lateran Council of 1215 had forbidden approval of any more new rules, but both Francis and the Carmelites had obtained verbal approval for their rules prior to the council.

Apparently owing to harassment by the Moslems, the hermits of Mt. Carmel were forced to leave the Holy Land and migrate West in the late 1230's and early 1240's. We can assume they did not leave their beloved Mt. Carmel without much hesitation! Even though they were given support for this move by Innocent IV (1200–54) in 1247, they were not initially well received in Europe. It seems that in an age when the apostolic zeal of the mendicants was sweeping across Europe, people simply did not understand the presence of a new order of contemplative hermits. They were neither monks not mendicants. Nor did they belong to an established group of hermits. Despite their approval by the church, many doubted both their authenticity and their orthodoxy. Something had to be done if they were to survive.

It was in light of this dilemma that the Carmelites shifted from the strictly eremitical to the mendicant model. Following the example of the Franciscans and the Dominicans, the Carmelites sought and obtained papal approval to adapt their eremitical rule to the apostolic life of mendicant poverty and itinerant preaching.

This was not easy, but it was not impossible. The Carmelite rule already encouraged an apostolic poverty that forbid the hermitage to possess "places or possessions, that is, houses or revenues." Thus, the common monastic practice of possessing much income-producing land and property was forbidden by their rule. In this the Carmelites were already very close to the strict poverty of the mendicant orders.

Furthermore, there were great debates within the community concerning this essential change in their lives. Were they hermits or friars? Were they to pray or to preach? Were they to live in isolated hermitages or in the midst of the city? These were all questions that faced this migrant community as it sought to survive in the West. It was in response to these questions that the book, *The Fiery Arrow*, was published to call the Carmelites back to their contemplative and eremitical origins.

After much struggle and time the Carmelites took their place within the mendicant orders of the West. Along with the Franciscans and the Dominicans, they began a life of apostolic poverty and itinerant preaching that took them from their beloved eremitical life into the bustling activity of the cities. However, even there the Carmelites held on to their hermit origins and maintained a strong contemplative tradition through the centuries. St. John of the Cross and St. Teresa of Avila (1515–82) in the sixteenth century are examples of the many men and women who have propagated this contemplative core to their apostolic works. In this reform they shared much in common with the reform of the fiery Franciscan, Peter of Alcantara (1499–1562), St. Teresa's spiritual director.

Through it all the Carmelites continued to profess a rule, or way of life, that was intentionally eremitical. They adapted and mitigated it, but its eremitical core remained. In our own time as Carmelites follow the admonition of Vatican II to return to their origins, they join all of us who are presently discovering our eremitical and contemplative roots. Along with us all, especially those of us who draw strongly from the mendicant explosion of the thirteenth and fourteenth centuries, they join us as we try to bring the hermitage of the past into the present and as we build for the contemplative church of the future!

Carmelite eremitism integrates the written formality of an approved rule of the church with the loose-knit informality of the Oriental, eremitical colony. It integrates the East and the West, the hermit and the mendicant, and the contemplative and the apostolic worker. In this the Carmelites speak with a profound voice in the whole eremitical movement of our time.

The Augustinians

Contrary to what their title indicates, the Augustinians were not founded by any one founder. They are actually a composite of many separate communities who profess the rule of St. Augustine. These communities include the Canons Regular, the Dominicans, and the Augustinians. The latter were actually founded by the Great Union of 1256 in which separate communities of hermits who professed the rule of St. Augustine were united under the title "The Order of Hermits of St. Augustine." It was only in the twentieth century that this title was officially dropped in favor of simply "The Order of Augustine."

The Augustinians trace their origins to four major groups of hermits. Each one of these communities was autonomous and independent, with its own founder or founders and history. Likewise, they developed in their own set of local circumstances.

The Williamites were founded by St. William of Maleval (d. 1157). He had no desire to found an order or write a rule, but sought only to live a life of solitary prayer. It was only after his death that one of his followers, Albert, wrote the *Customs and Rule of St. William.* In the years that followed the Williamites grew throughout Italy, France, Belgium, Germany, Bohemia, and Hungary. They were known as the Order of St. William.

It seems that their organization did not grow in proportion to their numbers. The Williamites had no central government, no superior general, and no regular chapters. This left room for much pluralism, but it also led to confusion within the community. The church then began to intervene. In 1237, Gregory IX, the friend of St. Francis, mitigated the rigor of their lives and imposed the moderate *Rule of St. Benedict* on them, with the customs of the contemplative Cistercians. Apparently this did not work out so well, for Innocent IV began urging them to follow the example of the mendicant communities, alternating between the hermitage and the apostolate. This led to further confusion. Were they hermits or mendicant friars? At this point some of the communities broke away from the motherhouse's frail and new centralized government. Apparently, some began to incorporate into a congregation of hermits in Tuscany and professed the rule of Augustine.

It was at this point that the papal legate, Cardinal Richard Annibaldi, began to include the Williamites in his plan for the "Great Union." Although the Order of St. William sent delegates to the Roman chapter for the Great Union, and even accepted its conclusions, the order did not accept the decision of its delegates. What followed was a long series of debates and negotiations between the Williamites who had come to profess the *Rule of St. Benedict* and the rule of Augustine. Suffice to say that those who followed Benedict retained their autonomy, and those who followed Augustine were eventually incorporated into the Great Union.

"The Hermits of the Order of St. Augustine of Tuscany" grew out of one of the most fertile areas for the hermit movement of all Europe. These groups were very informal and had little or no contact with one another. With the Fourth Lateran Council they were required to organize from colonies to communities, with regular chapters, obedience to a major superior, and profession of an existing rule. Many of the hermit colonies of Tuscany requested the rule of St. Augustine.

With this the organizing Cardinal Annibaldi included them in the Great Union. As we will see, with the Great Union came definite favors from Rome, which encouraged the hermits to pass over to the mendicant life of the friars. However, the Hermits of the Order of St. Augustine of Tuscany alternated between their hermit life and the apostolic life with ease, so that they grew in numbers very quickly. Soon they had houses scattered throughout Europe.

"The Hermits of Brother John the Good" began like most of the rest—humbly, with no real intention of founding an order. John Bono simply lived a holy life in a hermitage and attracted followers. There was no rule, no organization other than the teachings of John. As the number of his followers increased he personally dealt with temporal problems with the wisdom of a "wise fool." In time, however, with the founding of new hermitages, some of his followers approached Rome to request the rule of St. Augustine, and Rome complied. John chose to resign his office and devote all of his time to prayer and lay preaching.

Ironically, these hermits had some problems with the Franciscans. It seems that they all wore a similar habit. This was also the case with other independent hermit groups in the Marches. To avoid confusion, those who professed the rule of Augustine changed to a black tunic, cincture, shoes, and a staff. The Franciscans wore gray or brown with a cord, no shoes, and a staff.

In time this group of hermits was also included in the Great Union. Like all the others they began undertaking more apostolic work and met with great success.

"The Hermits of Brettino" had no one founder, but were simply a group of devout hermits who joined together at the beginning of the thirteenth century. Perhaps because of a lack of any one charismatic individual, these hermits developed an organized government with relative speed and ease. In 1227, Gregory IX put them under papal protection. The next year they chose to profess the Augustinian rule. By 1235 they had a complete set of constitutions approved by the pope. They had a well-thought out government and a very zealous community which embraced a poverty very similar to that of the Franciscans.

These hermits also had a dispute with the Franciscans about their habit. It too was similar to the garb of the Friars Minor. Apparently, they wore no cincture and rejected the idea of a black habit. Only after their incorporation into the Great Union would they hesitantly accept the black tunic and cincture to avoid confusion.

It is no surprise, then, that perhaps the *Little Flowers of St. Francis* is one of the more helpful sources in describing the life and spirituality of these hermits. Although they professed different rules, they were much animated by the same spirit and ideal which was essentially a radical following of Christ as simple hermit-friars.

There were other hermit groups that also joined in the Great Union, but the above are the main ones. The essential point is this: The Augustinians have primarily eremitical origins. It was only after the process of the Great Union that the hermits began to take on the apostolic, mendicant life and eventually lose their eremitical nature almost entirely.

This move from hermit to friar is not necessarily out of the healthy rhythm of the Spirit as it was moving in those times. As we have seen, the hermits of that era were also itinerant preachers and pilgrims. They simply shared the graces of God they found in the hermitage with a world thirsty for God. They stood in contrast to the exclusivity of the Western monks, and were at once more prayerful and more available to the average person. They were more radically rooted in the literal imitation of Christ as their primary model.

It comes as no surprise, then, that when Rome encouraged these communities of hermits to undertake apostolic activity, they quickly and easily complied. It was not necessarily seen in conflict with the eremitical ideal of the time. Furthermore, the success of the Franciscans had popularized this "mixed life" and made it acceptable to Rome.

It is with this in mind that we include the Augustinians in this study of the Franciscan hermitage. Like the Franciscans, they were part of the mendicant movement of the thirteenth and fourteenth centuries. Also, like the Franciscans, they had strong eremitical beginnings and would share in the heated recollect and descalced reforms of the sixteenth century which swept through the Franciscans, Carmelites, and Augustinians.

Perhaps the Augustinians have most in common with the founding of the Third Order Regular of St. Francis. In contrast to the Order of Friars Minor, the Third Order Regular was founded not by one founder, but by many preexisting communities coming together as one united order in 1447. Like the Augustinians, the Great Union was made up of many groups of hermits. Only after the union did they begin taking on the strongly mendicant model.

Hence the Augustinians and the Third Order Regular of St. Francis share much in common. Both began as hermits. Both went out from the hermitage to share the gospel of Jesus Christ with all the world. Both were very successful. Now both must rediscover their roots of eremitism if they are to continue to grow strong and full in the visible action of apostolic service.

There were, of course, other groups that made up the mendicant movement, but it was mainly the Carmelites and Augustinians who, along with the Franciscans, emphasized the hermit life. Though they all put the integration between contemplative solitude and apostolic action together in unique ways, and developed according to unique historical circumstances, they all still share much in the basic realities and tensions of this integration. These realities and tensions remain universal challenges for any group of hermits who seek to live the eremitical life as a formal community and in literal imitation of the gospel of Jesus Christ.

Let us now look more specifically into the eremitical life of Francis and the Franciscans.

8

THE FRANCISCAN HERMITAGE

⚬

One of the most difficult tasks in forming an understanding of the Franciscan hermitage is the near impossibility of being able to "formulate" the spirituality of St. Francis himself. There are of course Franciscan "rules," Franciscan biographies and histories, and even authentic writings of Francis, all of which are invaluable in coming to an understanding of the ideals of both the early movement and the man. But even with these historical and objective guides to early Franciscan spirituality, Francis of Assisi ever remains a mystical enigma to the logical modern mind. Being a true charismatic instrument of the Spirit, Francis was like the wind that blows wherever it wills, without human logic being able to discern fully its origins, its course, or its actual goal. Yet it is the steady blowing of this divine wind that changes the shape of a mountain and causes powerful storms to rise up from the oceans. Likewise, the divine and mystical madness of Francis of Assisi forever changed the shape of humankind, being surpassed only by the person of Jesus Christ, whom Francis himself so radically sought to imitate.

It is nonetheless helpful to investigate the "rule of life" for the hermitage in order to acquire at least some understanding of the structure and lifestyle of the Franciscan hermit community—as Francis himself envisioned it. Furthermore, some brief investigation of early biographical sources reveal how the communities themselves lived out in practical application Francis's eremitical "rule."

It should be understood that the early Franciscan life was a life of itinerancy. Owning nothing, the friars had no place to rest their heads in literal imitation of Christ. They wandered from place to place in obedience to St. Francis, alternating between work among the poor and solitary sojourns in the wooded hills and mountains. Their "hermitages" were caves or waddle huts, used as temporary dwellings on land they did not own. It was only after the passing of years that Francis saw the need to establish fixed dwellings for his itinerant hermit friars, who were often in need of places for quiet prayer. Even then the dwellings remained only three or four huts or caves scattered around a simple common house, and perhaps a small chapel. They refused ownership to these waddle-hut hermitages. Francis is said to have founded almost twenty-five of these hermitages.

One of the first things we notice when we read Francis's *Religious Life in Hermitages* is the "littleness" in both the length of the "rule" and in the size of this Franciscan colony of hermits. This informal "rule" is short, and the number of envisioned members is small. Francis says briefly and concisely that not more than three or four at most should be in the hermit colony. This smallness speaks immediately of the vocation of being a "lesser brother" within the greater church. Francis simply did not seek to rival his monastic forerunners. He sought only to give some minimal guidelines and structures to help his intimate family of spiritual brothers to pray. That is what his hermitage was for, and nothing more.

This smallness in number also indicates Francis's desire that the hermitage be a place where intimate personal relationships between little brothers in Christ could be nurtured, grow, and prosper. Instead of being a place to escape the responsibilities of a brotherly relationship born of Christian community, the small hermitage of Francis's little "rule" is seen as a gospel family of prayer, where relationship with Jesus is fostered and relationships with one's brothers is practically perfected in the mystically experienced love of Jesus Christ.

However, this fraternal dimension of the communal family is not seen as a compromise of the solitary rigor of the eremitical ideal. Francis says clearly that two of the brothers are to act as "mothers" and the other two, or one, are to act as their "children." These "children" are to be left free to live the pure and unemcumbered contemplative life of prayer in almost total solitude and silence; while the "mothers" are actively to take care of the daily needs of their contemplative children. Thus, the "mothers" are to lead the life of Martha, the servant, while the "children" are to lead the life of Mary, the contemplative. A very strict solitude and silence is thus tenderly and lovingly preserved for the solitary hermit-child who seeks but to sit at the feet of Jesus, his Savior and Lord.

This unusual terminology of "mother" and "child" further manifests Francis's tender and existential heart speaking beyond words of a cosmic mystery, both utterly simple and deeply profound. It is in the midst of solitude that we discover the spiritual family of God. Thus the hermitage is a place where the Word will lead us into the desolation of solitary silence, but the solitary silence will show us how to console our divine family with healing and life-giving words of Christ's experienced love.

While couching this initial objective ideal of integration between solitude and community in such informal and heart-melting personal terms, Francis goes on to give some very brief and practical guidelines for the structuring of the solitary life in the hermitage. He states clearly that each hermit is to have a separate cell or enclosure to insure the privacy needed for undistracted prayer and contemplation. He goes on to say that the hermits should not be forced to sleep together in one room, thus insuring that the dormitory style of life as practiced by the cenobitic monks of that time be totally absent in the hermitage. The dormitory of the cenobitic monastery was a large room where large numbers of monks all slept and lived together, living in contemplative silence, but living and sleeping in almost constant contact with their brother-monks and closely resembling a military barracks.

The Franciscan hermit's enclosure and cell was also to be kept totally free of outsiders by the active and loving intervention of the "mothers." Yet even the "mothers" were to avoid almost all contact with the outside world. All this was done to insure an environment of maximum silence and solitude, where the contemplative life could be fully lived by both the Marthas and the Marys of the Franciscan hermitage.

Conversely, Francis speaks clearly about the structured community life of togetherness within the hermitage. Francis insists that the eremitical "child" should have the ordinary freedom of poor people to speak at appointed times. Yet, even then he may speak only to his "mother." Through this reference to "begging alms" from the mothers, Francis is probably suggesting that this speech be loving and tender, but only when necessary to meet the real needs of the contemplative hermit. By saying that the hermits are "forbidden to take their meals" in their private enclosures, or cells, it seems that the practice of sharing meals in common was the custom even in the hermitage. However, silence was almost certainly maintained during these meals, as was the religious custom of the day. It is also interesting that Francis would give us his most exact description of common liturgical prayer in his description of the life in the Franciscan hermitage. In the hermitage, the divine office was apparently one of the standards for establishing a rhythm between solitude and community, between silence and proper speech. Whether or not the canonical prayer hours were prayed in common or in private is not totally clear, but at least we know that this liturgical emphasis keeps the view of the Franciscan hermit always within the context of a very real concept of community. During common liturgical prayer this becomes a profound, mystical reality, even if prayed in the privacy of one's own cell, while an actual gathering of the community more visibly gives outer witness to this interior, spiritual mystery.

That this particular and solitary dimension of the Franciscan life should be seen within the context of the greater Christian and Franciscan community is indicated by Francis's reference to the visit from the *custos*. This *custos* was the local or provincial minister of the entire Franciscan community of an area. The fact that he could choose to visit the hermitage indicates that the informal life of the hermitage was formally subject to the government and a real part of the lifestyle of the entire Franciscan body.

Yet, the particular informality of the hermitage is like a precious spiritual pearl and should not be quickly overlooked for fear that it might be lost. It should be noted that the internal "government" of the hermit colony is never formally mentioned. Only the concept of the servanthood of the "mothers" is mentioned. Cutting to the heart of the possibility of abusing the rules of "mother" or "child," Francis further says that the roles should be exchanged from time to time. However, in true Franciscan informality, our seraphic father says only that this should be done "now and then" and "according to whatever arrangement seems best suited for the moment." Thus, a real Spirit-led flexibility was really possible in the hermitage of a community that sought the Spirit himself as the primary minister of the entire order.

Other biographical sources indicate are even greater flexibility in living the eremitical life in various Franciscan places and environments. For instance, from Celano (d. 1260) we learn how the friars in Spain lived in "a certain poor hermitage." From the wording about how half the brothers took care of the domestic needs and half lived in contemplation, and how on one occasion all but one of the contemplatives "came together" for the common meal, it seems that there were more contemplatives in this hermitage than in the "two or one" called for by Francis. Furthermore, it seems that the tardy contemplative brother was lovingly left at peace to pray and experience the solitary, mystical graces of God, rather than being legalistically forced to attend the community meal. Thus, the legitimate need for prayer remained the sole criterion for both the size and the lifestyle of the community.

From Francis's own life in places that we know to be hermitages, we can perceive even more human insights into this communal, spiritual life of solitary prayer. We know that the "enclosure" of the contemplatives usually amounted to small, primitive huts or caves, grouped at random or by nature around a small chapel and common area as at the Carceri and Alverna. Thus, a great degree of freedom was apparently left to the solitary individual as to where and how to use his time. We know that Francis himself spent much time outside his cell in the vast expanse of nature. It seems that the early hermits were constantly praying "in the woods." Thus, it was sometimes difficult to have a conversation with a hermit, if the hermit was rapt in ecstasy in the middle of a dense forest, nowhere to be found. This, of course, happened to Francis himself when he went to have a spiritual conversation with his contemplative brother, Bernard. We also know that Bernard himself was apt to wander for weeks at a time in the densely wooded hills and mountains around a hermitage. Thus, Bernard probably entered into very little of the community discipline prescribed by Francis during these mystical pilgrimages of his free spirit.

We also know that at Greccio common meals were the custom, as prescribed in the "rule," for Francis rebukes the luxury of the friars' common table at Easter by coming to their door as a beggar. Yet from this we can also discern that it was probably the custom of this hermitage to give food to beggars during the common meal, thus seeing a flexible and charitable adaptation of Francis's strict prohibition of outsiders in the hermitage.

That both contemplative prayer and healthy community were vitally important to life in the hermitage is seen in the stories of how Francis sometimes did not show up for the community meal. Rapt up unto God, Francis would often be left to fast and pray. Likewise, if Francis was in the midst of a mystical trial or temptation and could not be a cheerful presence with his brothers, he would often stay in his cell to do battle with the powers of darkness, rather than inflict this darkness on the common life of the community.

Of course, this balance between private, mystical rapture and communal sensitivity are always present in Francis's spiritual life. It seems that during his frequent solitary sojourns "in the woods," Francis would allow his whole being to be rapt unto God, expressing himself freely through bodily motions and sounds. Yet, during his public prayer, Francis was always sensitive to the needs of the community in which he found himself, thus keeping his private experiences concealed, unless it was edifying to share them. This approach most assuredly applies to the hermitage.

From the real experience of places such as Poggio, Greccio, the Portiuncula, and even Alverna, it seems evident that apostolic preaching and work were not totally absent from the life of the hermitage. In fact, in the letters of Jacques de Vitry the early Franciscans are described as engaging in apostolic labors during the day and returning to their hermitages to pray at night.

It is a fact of Franciscan history that nearly every "apostolic sign" we popularly associate with Francis of Assisi took place either in or around the hermitage in which he himself was dwelling. Even his call of conversion to "rebuild my house" took place in the solitude of the "hermitage" of San Damiano. His greeting of peace took place outside the hermitage of Poggio. The entrance of all new members and the sending out of the first Franciscan missions took place in the cradle of the order, the Portiuncula, which was itself an adapted hermitage. Furthermore, the Portiuncula indulgence was seen as a very real ministry to the people of Francis's time from a place of strict solitude, silence, and prayer. The Christmas crib also originated at the hermitage of Greccio. The Canticle of the Creatures was composed during Francis's stay in a hermit's hut at San Damiano. Finally, Francis received the stigmata during the culmination of his mystical desire for intimate union with the suffering of Christ while staying in the hermitage of Alverna. Even from there Francis continued to go forth and preach to the people even though his weakened condition had deprived him of the physical vitality of his youth. In light of these early testimonies, it seems certain that some apostolic work was permitted for the brothers living in the hermitage.

Integrations between solitude and community, silence, and even the cloister and the world are all evident in the early lifestyle of the Franciscan hermitage. Francis put these integrations together in a way that was nothing short of revolutionary for his time, yet he retains the radical return to strict and simple gospel living, which places him squarely within the ever-developing tradition of Christian eremitism.

Of course, all of these flexible integrations were not without their problems of personal interpretation and abuse within the order. As any good Franciscan knows, "Franciscan flexibility" has been used as a justification for any luxury or self-indulgent abuse. Consequently, Francis had to emphasize that the "rule" for hermits should be observed with eagerness and zeal. He frequently corrected the idleness of the so-called contemplatives who turned holy leisure into a self-indulgent rest home for sluggards. Likewise, he constantly warned against the abuses against holy poverty within the hermitage, emphasizing especially that the friars should always wander as pilgrims in the "cloister" of the world within the "cell" of their bodies. Furthermore, he continued to warn those engaged in apostolic preaching to remember the dangers of pride that come with too much knowledge and too much fame. He states emphatically that it is the hidden prayers of the hermits which actually give power to the preacher's words and convert sinners, rather than the actual skill or human activity of the apostolic preacher. So while Francis permits a revolutionary freedom for the hermits of his order, he is quick to warn and correct abuses that eventually came with this freedom.

9

FRANCISCAN SAINTS
AND MOVEMENTS

Ꮼ

One of the best ways to discern the living reality of a divinely oriented spirituality is to look to the lives of the
real people within the movement. This is especially true of Franciscanism, which so strongly emphasizes the continuing incarnational dimension of the work of the person of Jesus Christ within
the lives of the people of God. Francis and his movement must be
studied from a personalized perspective, always seeing the Father's
working in real people as a highly dynamic and living reality of the
wind of the Spirit. Thus, in studying the life of Franciscan hermitages it will help us greatly if we study some of the lives of the
great men and women of the Franciscan movement who have been
powerful instruments of Spirit-led renewal and reform.

Shortly after the death of St. Francis, a major crisis faced the entire
order. As that order expanded, it rightly rose to meet the immediate
needs of the church in many ways. One of the most obvious ways
of renewing and reforming the church was for many of the brothers
to become priests and deacons. However, this meant that the lay
brothers would have to go to schools and universities in order to
be properly educated and trained in theology before they were ordained. This migration of many of the brothers into the university
towns for study caused a major shift from the original emphasis of
the Franciscan community. Where once a little mountain hermitage

life of contemplative prayer and loving labor served as the basis for the radical life of gospel simplicity, it was now necessary to set up large houses of study, which in turn involved the use of many books, the appropriation of proper study conditions, and the eventual use even of money and servants to staff the houses. Likewise, many educated clerics who came into the order felt the need to continue these conditions in order to minister properly to the very real and grave doctrinal problems of the day. Those who came into the priesthood after having first become Franciscan brothers often shared these clerical sentiments.

To the simple lay brothers who chose to stay in the little mountain hermitages to live a life of gospel poverty and contemplative prayer, this overall clericalization was seen as an abuse of the pure Franciscan ideal. It is true that Francis emphasized prayer before knowledge and poverty before "suitable conditions for learning." It is also true that much of this clericalization and the laxity which it fostered was an abuse of the pure ideals of St. Francis. Yet, even Francis admitted that as long as devotion and prayer were emphasized and maintained, the brothers could learn theology in order better to preach the Word of God. What was important to Francis was that the order properly grow and develop without compromising either gospel poverty or contemplative prayer. Unfortunately, many of the lay brothers from the hermitages failed to recognize this rightful development of the order within the overall church; so they wrongly condemned all learning and all clericalization.

What further complicated the issue was the inability for the well-intentioned but uneducated and simple lay brothers properly to discern the popular preaching and teaching that was spreading like wildfire through the Italy of their day. Unfortunately, much of this teaching was overly antichurch, anticlerical, and in nature highly eschatological. Consequently, the proper concern and disappointment of the lay brothers in the hermitages about abusive clericalism within the order soon turned to improper exclusivism and paranoic criticism when coupled with these heretical teachings. Needless to say, the brothers of the hermit life were soon seen as much a threat to the orthodoxy of the order as the clerics were seen as a threat to its purity.

Of course, all these circumstances only widened the gap between the two groups until the situation became a major crisis that threatened the very existence of the order of "lesser brothers." This was the "dynamite" that threatened to split the order apart—from the inside out!

St. Bonaventure (1221–74)

St. Bonaventure was the simple and prayerful Franciscan scholar and administrator who came on the scene to bring God's salvation to the order, at least temporarily. Bonaventure was very truly the ideal of the prayerful and peaceful Franciscan scholar. Being a budding scholar upon his entrance into the order, he soon became a contemplative mystic as well. It is from the mystical solitude of the hermitage of La Verna that he composed his most highly mystical work, the *Itinerarium Mentis in Deum.* This mystical work is seen by many as one of the most beautiful works of the thirteenth century.

During his tenure as minister general of the order, Bonaventure spent much time visiting the little mountain hermitages to acquaint himself with their simple lifestyle, so as to effect a better unity of both administration and experience within the divided Franciscan Order. It is from these hermitage experiences that Bonventure collected material from Francis's surviving first followers in order to write a good, balanced, official biography of the saint of Assisi. In this biography, Bonaventure attempted to retain and promote the purity of the simple hermitage ideal, while still leaving room for proper study in order to promote doctrinal purity. In these things he always sought a balance between prayer and study, between the hermits and the clerics.

Typically, when Bonaventure was given the news that he had been named cardinal bishop of Albano in 1273, this Franciscan mystic and scholar was busy washing dishes in a small mountain hermitage. This necessitated hanging his new cardinal's hat on the branch of an olive tree outside until he could finish the chores of the "mother" of the hermitage. The cardinal's hat hanging on the olive tree has thus become the recognized symbol of St. Bonaventure's work within the church and the order.

As a cardinal rooted in prayer, study, and community life, Bonaventure was able to bring about a great reconciliation between Eastern and Western Christendom during the Council of Lyons. However, Bonaventure died unexpectedly before this full work of unity was completed. In both the East and the West, however, St. Bonaventure won for himself the title "Seraphic Doctor of the Church."

To some readers it might seem unusual or even improper that we should include a reference to St. Bonaventure when studying the Franciscan hermitage life. However, it was St. Bonaventure who was primarily responsible for reconciling the hermits and the clerics, thus keeping a balanced expression of the hermitage within the developed tradition of the Franciscan order. It was owing to Bonaventure's personal experience of both the hermitage lifestyle and the clerical lifestyle that he was able to appreciate personally the need for both within the Franciscan tradition. It was due to his keeping this vital dimension of the Franciscan charism alive within the order that the pure Franciscan hermitage lifestyle persisted into the overall renewal of the entire order in years to come. Furthermore, Bonaventure's ability to be a peacemaker and a reconciler within the order and the church should not be seen aside from the fact that Bonaventure himself had first experienced this mystical peace, which passes all understanding, spending long hours in prayerful contemplation and humble brotherly service within the simple Franciscan hermitage.

Of course, human nature being what it is, the Franciscano, in the years following the inspiration of St. Bonaventure, fell back into their old abuses, and problems again arose. This was inevitable because Bonaventure was able to establish only a fragile peace and unity. Even during Bonaventure's time some of the extremists were never brought into the full unity or brotherly peace of the "reform." Bonaventure was a genius at integrating opposites into a creative communal whole, yet this integration made him a moderate rather than either a purist or a laxist. Consequently, the extremists again became active in spreading their factitious "poison" in the years shortly after Bonaventure's influence. Yet Bonventure's reform had been firmly established in Franciscan tradition and communal policy, and there was cause to remain hopeful and optimistic about similar crises within the Franciscan family of the future.

Paul of Trinci (1309–90)

Paul of Trinci is often seen as the founder of the Observant reform within the Franciscan family. While friars such as Bernardine of Siena (1380–1444), James of the Marches (1393–1476), or John Capistran (1386–1456) are usually thought of as the powerful and glorious preachers of that reform, Paul of Trinci was the simple hermit–lay brother who slowly and patiently worked for reform even before it was popular to do so.

Paul was associated with the friars from the age of fourteen. Even at this youthful stage of his vocation, he was upset by the laxity and abuses he saw within the average friary life. He felt it his duty to

God and to the friars to voice his concern. However, the friars did not welcome his criticism; so Paul was punished (as was the custom of the day) for his criticism by the friars. At this point, Paul's father stepped in to take his son out of the community for fear he was not being treated fairly. Ironically, it was in his father's backyard that this rejected and humiliated lay brother lived the pure Franciscan life. Even without the title "Franciscan," Paul truly rediscovered the gospel poverty and contemplative prayer that is the spiritual strength of true Franciscan eremiticism.

A few years later, Paul visited a new Franciscan house of brothers living the strict observance at Bugliano. Paul must have been overjoyed to find even a small group of brothers living the Franciscan life of poverty and prayer in childlike purity. Paul joined the community, but it was dissolved by higher authorities in 1355.

Paul returned to the friary at Foligno to live in a typical nonreform Conventual community as a lay brother. Again, he sought to bring reform, but again received little or no support from the community. It must have been a hard time for Paul, who at forty-five years of age was but an insignificant lay brother within a substantially clericalized order, calling out for reform to ears deafened by laxity and abuse. However, in 1368, Paul was given permission by the newly elected minister general, Thomas of Frignano, to return to Brugliano to live the pure Franciscan life as he felt called by God to live it. This can very properly be seen as the historic founding date of the Observant reform.

At first Paul was forced by lack of support to live his simple life of prayer and poverty alone. In this solitude he undoubtedly grew from the experience of his roots when he was but a young, humiliated hermit, living in his father's backyard. However, in time news of his solitary holiness spread through the region, and brothers began to investigate his lifestyle seriously. A small group of brothers slowly formed around Paul at Trinci, calling themselves the "Brethren of the Family of the Observants."

The poverty of this group was truly extreme. They ate only bread and water, and the place in which they lived was said to be overrun by frogs and snakes. Because of the sharp rocks in and around the place, they could not go barefoot; so they made and wore "clogs" to protect their feet. It was from these "clogs" that they were given the name *Zoccolanti*. Eventually, other reform groups began to look to the *"Zoccolanti"* for inspiration and affiliation. In time Paul was looked upon as the informal leader of this entire new movement.

In 1373, Pope Gregory XI (1329–78) gave his formal approval to the Observant reform of Brother Paul. From that time on growth became more steady. Ten friaries were initially set aside to follow the literal "observance" of the pure Franciscan rule. These ten friaries included the traditional hermitages of Carceri, Greccio, Fonte Columbo, and Poggio Bustone. By 1389 the brothers had been given places in which to live the observance. Paul was looked upon by the pope, the minister general of the Franciscan Order, and the brothers of the reform as the undisputed guardian-general of this entire movement. In 1390, when Paul of Trinci died, he was a happy Franciscan hermit-preacher, having lived to see the beginnings of his dream for reform fulfilled within the Franciscan Order he loved so much.

Paul of Trinci differs from St. Bonaventure in many ways, yet both accomplished the reform of the developed but pure Franciscan life in their own time. Paul was a simple lay brother who came out of the hermitage experience in order to bring reform to a highly clericalized Franciscan community. Bonaventure was a scholar and a cleric who grew to love the simple hermit life—enough to keep it properly balanced and very much alive in the Franciscan tradition. Both were men deeply rooted in prayer and poverty, keeping the original fire of Francis of Assisi a living flame of mystical love burning brightly within both the church and the world.

Paul of Trinci was a man of simplicity, courage, and patience. He was a man who was able to live the Franciscan hermit life, even when he received no outside support from his community. Because he was a man of prayer, he found an interior support that kept him ever on course toward his final destiny. He did not seek to be a cleric or a founder, yet from his humility God raised him up as the founder of one of the strongest reforms in Franciscan history. His example should be an inspiration to every person who seeks the renewal of the simple hermit life within the Franciscan family.

James of the Marches (1394–1476)

One of the greatest Franciscan hermit-preachers of the Observant reform was James of the Marches. In his call to solitude, James first thought he should become a hermit with the Carthusians, but the Carthusians felt doubtful of his call to their community and told him to come back later in his life.

During this time James passed through Assisi and stayed at the Portiuncula with the Friars Minor. Touched by the gospel simplicity of the traditional Franciscan "mix," James was invested as a novice in this tiny hermitage which was looked upon as the "cradle of the Franciscan Order." He spent his novitiate, again in a hermitage environment, in the mystical solitude of the Carceri. Undoubtedly, it was during his novitiate at the Carceri that James grew to experience and love the Franciscan peace which passes all understanding.

James's lifestyle was a true attempt to return to the purity of the original ideals of St. Francis. He spent long hours in solitary prayer, during which he undoubtedly experienced the mystical graces of union with Christ. As a true lover of poverty, James lived an extremely austere and ascetical life, preparing himself through fasting and watchful prayer for the visitations of the Holy Spirit. Through the power of the Holy Spirit he received the charismatic gifts of prophecy and miracles. As the power of God overflowed from this hermitage-trained contemplative, James ventured forth in gospel freedom to preach the good news of Jesus to all the world. The effects of his preaching are life-changing miracles in themselves.

James was eventually offered the archbishopric of Milan as a result of his manifest wisdom in counseling both princes and popes. However, in the peaceful sureness of knowing his call to be but a simple Franciscan penitent, James of the Marches turned down the honor in order to live in unadorned humility. In November 1476, James of the Marches died a very simple and humble Franciscan, but a man who had truly been a powerful instrument of the Spirit of God in order divinely to change our human world for the better.

James of the Marches is a primary example of a simple hermit and humble cleric who preached the Word of God with Spirit-given power. He effectively lived the healthy, creative tension of the Franciscan "mix" between contemplation and action with the success that only God can give. James was always concerned with the spiritual good of a hermit, something he had learned so well during his time of training and formation in the beloved hermitage of the Carceri. Though remembered primarily for his preaching, James of the Marches was a "Franciscan hermit" in the true sense of the word.

Bernardine of Siena (1380–1444)

Bernardine of Siena was another great preacher of the Observant reform who spent much time in the great Franciscan hermitages such as the Carceri and La Speco di Narni. In fact, Bernadine was trained in Paul of Trinci's beloved hermitage of Brugliano. He became one of the unifying pillars of the Observant reform.

The Observant friars were an attempt to return to the original purity of the Franciscan life as it had been lived in the little mountain hermitages; they never were in favor of causing divisions within the order or the church. After Bonaventure's time of peaceful influence, the Spiritual party, who strongly advocated the hermit life, broke away from both the Franciscan Order and the Catholic Church, while the Observants of Bernardine's time were interested in true and radical reform—but never at the unnecessary expense of losing the gospel unity with the Conventual Franciscans. Likewise, though Bernardine was personally responsible for the reform of three hundred convents, he was constantly striving for a Christlike unity within the reform and within the entire Franciscan family, of which the reform was a part. When Bernardine was made vicar general of the Observants, he continued to strive for a spiritual and structural unity with both the Franciscan family and the entire church.

In his moderate and balanced approach to reformed lifestyle, Bernardine of Siena never sought the rigid poverty and exclusive solitude of the Spirituals' hermitage. On the contrary, he felt it was important to balance solitude with apostolic work and preaching. However, if these simple Franciscans were to preach, he felt they should preach the truth and preach the truth well! Consequently, Bernardine helped to establish a school of theology in Perugia to help his humble yet ever-popular friars to preach to and counsel with the simple people of his day.

Bernardine himself became one of the more popular preachers of his century, yet he was trained in the simple life of the hermitage. Being grounded and rooted in this mystically experienced simplicity, Bernardine's preaching was always aimed at helping simple people to live a prayerful yet practical Christian life. One such example was his preaching of the holy name and the use of the symbol "IHS" in order to rally the crowds to unity in Christ.

Common people of his day often formed into small secular groups that battled with one another over an endless list of civil issues. These issues were usually small and insignificant, but the violence that followed was usually scandalous, destroying the peace and order of small villages and large cities alike. Each of these groups usually rallied around a banner with a symbol on it. Consequently, as Bernardine uncompromisingly preached the gospel of Jesus' peace in order to reestablish both spiritual and civil peace and order, he likewise developed the use of the symbol "IHS" in order to unify people around the holy name to which every knee will eventually bow.

Because of the development and use of this unifying Christian symbol, Bernardine was accused of both heresy and idolatry. Bernardine of Siena, who had always lived, taught, and preached moderation, balance, and unity, was now brought to trial before the pope in Rome and accused of the exact opposite of what he believed, lived, and preached. Yet, Bernardine faithfully submitted to the due process of the church and defended himself with the humility and patience of a true little brother of St. Francis. Of course, he was found completely innocent during the papal trial, and both Pope Martin and Eugene IV spoke and wrote in Bernardine's behalf. He was offered the bishoprics of Siena, Ferrara, and Urbino, but like James of the Marches, he refused them in order to maintain his humility as a true Friar Minor.

Ironically, yet symbolically, Bernardine of Siena died in a Conventual friary at Aquila on May 20, 1444. Though he had fought many years for the success of the Observant reform, he never wanted to break the unity of the Franciscan family. Consequently, he and John Capistran tried constantly to keep a formal split from occurring with the Conventual Franciscans, yet through human rivalry and misunderstanding the split came anyway. In a symbol of the peace and unity Bernardine was always striving for, he went to be with the Lord through death while staying with the Conventual friars at Aquila. He was canonized by Nicholas V in 1450, and his basilica and shrine stand in Aquila where he died.

St. Bernardine of Siena stands out as a truly great man within the tradition of the Franciscan hermitage. He was a man rooted and formed in the solitude of the Franciscan eremitical life, yet he was a man ever concerned for the salvation of the whole world. Willing to give his life in order to establish a reform so that the Franciscan life of the gospel could be lived without compromise, Bernardine of Siena was also interested in preserving the unity and balance that full gospel living should bring. He sought solitude, yet he was one of the greatest preachers of his century. He sought reform, yet he always stood for moderation, balance, and unity with the rest of the Franciscan family and the church. When falsely accused, he responded with the peace and patience of Christ, by whose holy name he had brought peace and reconciliation to hundreds of thousands. Understandably, both the Observant reform he helped to establish and the "IHS" symbol of the holy name by which he promoted peace still stand as major symbols and communities within today's church.

The name of St. Bernardine of Siena will always be associated with the divine light of the holy name he both experienced in solitude and preached to the world.

Peter of Alcantara (1499–1562)

Another great reformer and integrator of the Franciscan ideal was Peter of Alcantara, the originator of the Alcantarine reform of the Observant friars. As is usually the case with all spiritual reforms, even the great Observant reform of Paul, James, and Bernardine was itself soon in desperate need of reform. Again, the ideals of poverty and prayer were the issues. Again, a reform of the reform was raised up through the power of the Spirit working in just a few solitary souls who were courageous enough to make themselves available to God by living a life of ascetic poverty and quiet, listening prayer. Peter of Alcantara was one of those men.

Highly educated, Peter soon understood the clerical approach to the Franciscan life after he joined the friars in 1515. However, as a member of the Observant branch of the Franciscan family, we can assume that the ideals of the founders of the reform burned deeply in his heart. After his ordination in 1524, Peter began a preaching apostolate to the poorest of the poor. Peter always showed a great devotion to the cross and a great sympathy for the human condition. Soon great numbers of lay people began to give their lives to Jesus and live the gospel without compromise. Being touched by the divine power of Christ who laid down his life for the poor on the cross, Peter began constructing large crosses at the parishes when he had concluded his mission of preaching so that the people would always be reminded of the love of God. Peter of Alcantara soon became a very popular friar, known for living the life of a Friar Minor and preaching the gospel of Jesus Christ without compromise.

In 1538, Peter was elected provincial of the St. Gabriel province. As provincial, he continued to live a very austere Franciscan life while assuming the responsibilities of organization and discipline. He also continued his successful preaching apostolate during this time. However, in 1540, Peter drew up a new set of constitutions for his province. Drawing on the tradition of the Observant family and his own experience, these constitutions strongly emphasized both poverty and prayer. Unfortunately, the friars of his province thought these constitutions much too severe. At this point, Peter of Alcantara joined the long line of reformers who form an unbreakable line all the way back to our father, Francis of Assisi, and humbly retired to the solitude of a hermitage to live the pure Franciscan life with just a few brothers.

This was, however, a new beginning and not an end. Brothers soon came streaming from all around the province, and in time many communities were reformed. In 1560, these reformed friaries were erected as a separate province under the name "The Living Image of St. Francis." During the pontificate of Julius III (1487–1555), Peter of Alcantara walked seven hundred miles barefooted to ask the pope for permission to establish houses around the world of the "strictest observance."

Like Peter himself, the Alcantarine reform was both popular and uncompromising. The convents and the cells within them were simple and small. Likewise, their churches were kept on a small scale and were quite simple. In further keeping with pure Franciscan poverty, none of this property was owned by the friars themselves. Lay people were the sole owners and keepers of the brothers' places. At the end of each year the brothers gave the keys to the buildings back to the owners, giving them the option to evict the friars from the premises. In keeping with Francis's warnings about the pride of scholarship and the wealth of owning books, the convents of the Alcantarine reform possessed no libraries. Only a few devotional books were allowed for each brother, thus placing an uncompromising emphasis on prayer rather than scholarship. The asceticism of the friars was likewise quite extreme. Their food and clothing were minimal to say the least, and they kept a rule of perpetual abstinence and constantly went barefoot. More than likely, it was owing to this passionate desire to embrace and know Jesus in one's whole body, soul, and spirit that the Holy Spirit moved with mystical power through both the lives and the preaching of these zealous Franciscan brothers.

The life of Peter of Alcantara seems very harsh to many modern Franciscans, yet the spiritual and organizational fruits of his life are undeniably positive. Especially in the area of mortification of his body, Peter seems almost masochistic to the modern Christian of the twentieth century. Like many of his Franciscan predecessors, he scourged his body with a cord to fight off physical lust, yet in this he was often drawn close to the physical experience of our crucified Lord. Toward the end of his life, he slept only one or so hours a night, and this he did while sitting erect on his floor rather than reclining in even a very poor Franciscan bed.

Even in the midst of these physical mortifications of the flesh, God did not allow Peter's body to weaken. Peter continued to exercise his preaching apostolate with power and success. Likewise, he gave spiritual direction to many people. One of these was the famous reformer of the Carmelite Order, St. Teresa of Avila. However, in his humility he denied himself the privilege of being the spiritual director of emperors and state leaders. With his experienced success as a spiritual director, Peter wrote a mystical treatise on prayer that is celebrated the world over as a masterpiece of mystical genius for his day and for ours.

As the leader of the Alcantarine reform, Peter's responsibilities were many and undeniably taxing; however, his skill as an organizer was and is obvious. Even in the midst of his fame and success, Peter never tired of performing the lowliest household tasks of the friaries in which he lived. Faithful in following Jesus and serving people in his mystical Body, Peter experienced a fullness of mystical and charismatic graces that included the miraculous. Often when experiencing the charismatic gifts of rapture and ecstasy, he would lose track of time or location, paying little attention to the church or surroundings where he might have been praying. He is said to have been unaware of whether a church where he prayed daily for years was roofed with a vaulted or flat roof.

As a true Franciscan "free spirit," Peter was known actually to travel through the air in levitation in order to pray at the foot of a cross. While praying he was often seen shining with a divine light much brighter than the sun. Undeniably Peter of Alcantara was a true Franciscan who was greatly empowered by the Spirit of God.

Peter of Alcantara has much to say to today's renewal of the hermit life of prayer within the Franciscan family. While not actually hermitages in the pure sense of the word, all the Alcantarine houses were truly houses of prayer. Likewise, while not every modern Franciscan house should be a hermitage, every Franciscan household should be a house of prayer if both the brothers and sisters and their apostolates are going to succeed in the full power of the Spirit of God. Furthermore, the Alcantarine emphasis on poverty and asceticism stands as a constant reminder that the "archaic" disciplines of our Franciscan fathers often brought forth a popular and personal spiritual renewal that often surpasses the present experience of the typical modern Franciscan. We modern Franciscans should constantly seek to prepare ourselves in body as well as in spirit for the divine visitations of the Spirit into our lives. If we faithfuly do this, then the message of Peter of Alcantara will continue to be heard and proclaimed in the Franciscan communities of toady's world.

It is not at all surprising that we find two famous reformers, St. Peter and St. Teresa, teaming up to renew the original idea of their founders within two integral communities of the church. Today, both St. Peter of Alcantara and St. Teresa of Avila cry out for a further cooperation and integration between the various eremitical and spiritual traditions of the church. Though some brothers and sisters might consider them only archaic examples of Tridentine Catholicism, St. Peter of Alcantara and St. Teresa of Avila symbolically call us all to a working and creative integration of past and present traditions that could truly be nothing short of a spiritual revolution of eremitism in the future.

Bonaventure of Barcelona (1620–89) and Leonard of Port Maurice (1676–1751)

Each of these two men represents a reform that grew alongside the Alcantarine reform of St. Peter. These reforms form a family called the *Riformella*. Like the Recollects of the same period, a heavy emphasis on making each friary a house of recollection, or prayer, places them undeniably within the developed Franciscan tradition of the hermitage.

Like John Capistran, Bonaventure of Barcelona entered the Order of Friars Minor after having lived in the secular world as a married man. Choosing to remain only a humble lay brother, Bonaventure soon went to Assisi and lived at San Damiano. It was more than likely that at San Damiano Bonaventure experienced the contemplative peace of St. Francis and St. Clare. Advancing in the mystical life, he soon heard a voice from God advising him to "Go to Rome and there fill my house with joy."

In Rome Bonaventure worked as a doorkeeper for awhile at St. Isadore's. Soon the call to live a more strict Franciscan life beckoned him. He responded by establishing St. Bonaventura at Palatino as a house of reform where the rule was to be lived "without gloss." There were many other brothers seeking a similar pristine Franciscan life; so other reform houses were soon formed. It was during this time that Bonaventure was made superior by the pope and commissioned to write constitutions for the growing new reform movement. Bonaventure's holy life, rooted in prayer and poverty, made him a popular spiritual counselor. Among those who sought his advice was no less than the pope. Here we have, again, a simple lay brother establishing a reform rooted in prayer and poverty that would affect the entire Franciscan order, the church, and the world.

Leonard of Port Maurice was a highly educated young man who joined the reform of Bonaventure of Barcelona in 1697, after consulting both the Jesuits and the Dominicans about his desire to be a Franciscan. It was during this time of formation that Leonard became acquainted with the life of quiet and prayer that characterized the life of the reform houses. After his ordination to the priesthood in 1703, he began a very popular preaching mission throughout Italy. However, even in the midst of this apostolic ministry, Leonard always rooted his life in Christ through long periods of contemplative solitude and a severe ascetical discipline. From this contemplative life of solitude he developed a passionate devotion to the cross of Jesus Christ. Having personally experienced the power of the cross in his life, Leonard of Port Maurice began to promote a popular devotion to the way of the cross by leading others in what we now call the "stations of the cross."

This balance between contemplation and action, centered on the cross, is strikingly symbolized at Fonte Columbo, the famous Franciscan hermitage where a sick and weakened Francis of Assisi struggled in solitude to give the brothers a rule truly inspired by the Spirit of God. It was at Fonte Columbo that Leonard of Port Maurice instituted the Way of the Cross, erecting actual stations along the road to the Sacro Speco (Sacred Cave) in 1745. It was in this very cave that Francis wrote the rule of 1223, which is so founded on living the cross of Jesus Christ.

With Leonard of Port Maurice we again see the authentic Franciscans "mix" lived out beautifully. A brother rooted in contemplative prayer and a true devotion to the cross, Leonard became one of the most popular preachers and spiritual directors in all of Italy. He counseled the rich and the poor, kings and paupers. He also established a popular devotion to the cross that would live in the church even until the present time. None of this power would have been experienced in his ministry had he not first experienced the power of the cross of Jesus personally through long hours of solitary prayer. This life was made possible for St. Leonard through the establishment of the reformed Franciscan community by a simple lay brother, Bonaventure of Barcelona. The Way of the Cross at Fonte Columbo stands out boldly as a striking symbol of both of these reformers' rootedness in the uncompromising approach to living the rule of St. Francis and the mystical paradox of the cross of Jesus Christ.

The Capuchin Reform

It would be a gross oversight to pass over the Capuchin reform and its founders when discussing Franciscan eremitism. Its direct eremitical emphasis in its foundation, plus its legacy of canonized and noncanonized saints, speak of its lasting place within the eremitical tradition of the Franciscan family and the entire church.

The Capuchins were founded through what at first appears to be a tragic comedy of errors between the reforming few and the institutional many. It all started when Matteo di Bassi (d. 1552) was given a vision of St. Francis through which he was inspired to adopt a more primitive Franciscan habit and observe the rule literally. Even though Matteo was already a member of the province of the Marches of the Observants, which was itself already aspiring to observe the rule literally as a reform province, he sought and gained individual approval from Clement VII, as long as he reported to his provincial superior annually. Unfortunately, Matteo did not receive this papal approval in writing, an oversight that he would later regret. Needless to say, the provincial was less than thrilled by this rather independent approach to reform. He put Matteo in prison. Matteo was released only through the intervention of his friend, Catarina Cyba, duchess of camerino, who was a relative of Pope Clement.

About the same time (1525) two brothers by birth, Ludovico and Raffaele da Fossombrone, also approached the provincial of the Marches to live the rule literally. Apparently this series of events angered the provincial minister, and he refused the request. From this point onward the same provincial minister took up a dogged opposition to the Capuchin reform. An ecclessiastical game of hide-and-seek ensued. Ludovico and Raffaele scurried off to seek refuge with the Conventuals at Cingoli. The provincial then obtained a written papal brief declaring Matteo, plus the two brothers, to be apostates, and led a band of Observant Friars to retrieve their absent brethren. The two brothers fled into the mountains and ended up taking refuge in a Camaldolese hermitage, a connection with profound effects on the shape of the reform yet to come. So well did the brothers take to this eremitical life that they actually sought to join the Camaldolese. The monks wisely refused. Matteo, who had already been imprisoned once by this law-and-order provincial, was content to continue wandering free as an individual itinerant preacher.

Matteo's personal peace was soon disturbed by the two brothers, who sought him out with a brief from the grand penitentiary authorizing them and Matteo to pursue their dream, yet together as members of the Observants. They were therefore grouped together. Matteo's freedom as an itinerant was over. But the damage was done. There was "bad blood" between these few reforming friars and the Observants, especially the provincial of the Marches. Under the civil protection of the duchess they sought church protection from the Conventual minister general, who acceded to their request. But this was, at best, a questionable canonical position. So the duchess again approached her uncle, Pope Clement VII, and persuaded him to protect this new group. On July 3, 1528, the pope issued a bull that founded the Capuchin Order.

It would be good to mention, at least in passing, that the Conventuals themselves had a reform movement underway about this same time in response to the still new Observant reform. It does seem strange that, in the midst of this reform in all the branches of the First Order, there was so much rivalry and dissension. Is it not strange how leery reformers are of one another? Perhaps if they had just worked together a little more, so much grief could have been avoided.

The "Capuchins" was not the original name of the group. "Friars Minor of the Eremitical Life" was their first official name. It is only with the passing of time that the more popular name of "Capuchin" would be used, a name first used by children when describing the hood of the friars' distinctive habit. So, the original name itself is intentionally both Franciscan and hermitical.

Some would say that the Capuchin habit was itself the habit of the pilgrim hermit. The hood was pyramidal, or pointed, and was attached to the tunic. The traditional hood of the itinerant pilgrim-hermit of the penitential tradition was the same, and was so recognized by the people. It is not, by the way, surprising that St. Francis himself wore the penitential garb of a hermit at the beginning of his conversion. We might well suppose that he kept at least the hermit's hood when he exchanged his leather belt for a simple cord and cast off his shoes to wander unshod or in sandles at best. In this both the original habit of St. Francis and the habit of the first Capuchins was hermitical.

The prayer life of the reform also reinforces their eremitical nature. The Capuchins' first statutes actually declare that contemplation is *the* reason for the reform. Apostolic action is only skeptically permitted, an attitude not entirely in line with authentic Franciscan eremitism. Furthermore, they were to spend a full four hours daily in private prayer beyond community prayer. This might be done in chapel, but an environment of privacy and solitude were to be maintained even in the chapel where all windows were closed so as to shut out exterior light and distractions. Their choral office shows the distinct mark of the Camaldolese reform of Monte Carona. The chant was to be strictly unsung—no music, with plain diction and stark simplicity. Here, too, they seem to have adopted a more Camaldolese than authentic Franciscan approach. In later years much of this would be changed, but not without some struggle.

It is of definite interest that Ludovico's leadership role further identifies the eremitical nature of this reform. This is true not only in his almost one-sided insistence on the eremitical contemplative dimension, but also in his role in moderating the reclusive excesses of individual friar-hermits. It seems that some overzealous hermits were becoming ill and actually dying from excessive fasting and bodily mortification. It is Ludovico who insisted on "monastic solitude" rather than individual, or individualistic, solitude. In this he manifests the more positive side of the Camaldolese influence in his own spirituality.

The actual layout of the first hermitages was definitely eremitical. While there was a rigorous emphasis on poverty in an attempt to return to Franciscan origins, there was also an emphasis on being situated in solitude outside of urban centers. While this is not overly "un-Franciscan," the emphasis of Francis seemed to be more one of defining how "near" to people the hermitages should be rather than how far "removed." The actual distance was much the same. There was the institution of one or two isolated cells where friars could engage in more intense solitude. While it would be incorrect to compare strictly the layout of the Capuchin places to those of the Camaldolese, many see a strong Camaldolese connection here because of Ludovico's personal desire for solitude and his sojourn with the Camaldolese during his flight from the Observant provincial. However, even a basic study of the "places" of Francis proves that the cells of the first friars were also what we would now call hermitages. Again, it is more a question of attitude rather than actual action that constitutes the Camaldolese influence with the first Capuchins.

We can begin to learn some very tragic lessons from the examples of some important Capuchins. The first, and most important, is from Ludovico himself. Having been voted out of his office of leadership, the next chapter of 1536 began to moderate some of the one-sided eremitical emphases that were the direct result of Ludovico's personal attitudes, plus his rather dictatorial approach to leadership. The chapter did this by placing a proper balancing emphasis on the apostolate as well as on contemplation, and by reducing the mandatory time for personal and private prayer from four hours to two hours daily.

Ludovico himself responded to the growing resistance to his dictatorial reign by refusing to submit to his lawfully elected successor, Benedine d'Asti, in 1535. This resulted in his being expelled from the very order he helped to found. But he did not stop there, and went so far as to suggest to the chapter of 1536 that they give up all active ministry and preaching in order to retire into the strict seclusion of an eremitical life. It became painfully and sadly clear to all that Ludovico was not really called to the Franciscan way of life, but to an eremitism that was far more reclusive than Francis had ever desired for the brotherhood as a whole.

Matteo di Bassi was expelled from the order at about the same time, but for different reasons. Like Ludovico, Matteo also would not submit to the new vicar general. With Matteo it was not so much that he wanted to rule the order and direct it toward a strictly eremitical life, but because he simply wanted to live the life of an itinerant pilgrim-preacher as an individual without submitting to any community rule or discipline, except on his terms. Matteo was expelled from an order he did not really even try to found or join. We might rightly say it joined him in order to grow and then discarded him when it had outgrown him. Matteo stands as an example of a lone prophetic figure who probably should never have embraced community life at all.

Ludovico and Matteo stand as warnings of two extremes: Eremitism to the exclusion of apostolic activity, and the pilgrim life to the exclusion of community. Both eremitical seclusion and the life of a pilgrim-wanderer can be properly included in authentic Franciscan eremitism. However, neither can be seen as a primary model. Neither Ludovico nor Matteo were wrong in what they felt called by God to live. They were wrong, however, in expecting their personal approach to be the communal norm for all Franciscans. Ludovico might well have found peace in a more reclusive, eremitical community, and Matteo might have been better off as a lay penitent.

Both were problematic within an authentic Franciscan approach to eremitical life in the First Order tradition.

The third tragic figure is that of the apostasy of the fourth vicar general, Bernardino Ochino da Siena, in 1542. Bernardino was extremely popular throughout the world as both a preacher and a counselor. Yet he became so engrossed in his activities that he lost his base of contemplative prayer and the original eremitical life of the Capuchins. It was present in the legislation of the order, but it was not present in his own personal life. Bernardino left the order and the church and joined the Calvinists in 1542. His doctrinal defection was seemingly the direct result of a defection from the intentional eremitical life of prayer he orginally vowed. He stands as a stark warning of how far one can fall from grace if one does not take the time and provide the space to prayer. His activity ate up his prayer life until he fell from the very faith he so actively preached and professed. He is a tragic figure calling out to the "work'a'holic" friars and sisters of our own day who spend all their time preaching and legislating contemplative prayer and hermitical life, but never live it themselves.

The Capuchins say much both positively and negatively about the eremitical dimension of the Franciscan life. More than any other First Order community they intentionally stood, and continue to stand, for the eremitical ideal within the Franciscan way of life. Yet, they also warn us through the very founders they eventually expelled for extremes: eremitism to the exclusion of community, individual itineracy and pilgrimage to the exclusion of community, and activity to the exclusion of prayer. All stand as stark and distant warnings about the problems that face religious life today. Yet through all this the Capuchin example calls all Franciscans everywhere again to take seriously the call of the Spirit who always leads back to poverty and prayer in our own hermitages.

We have emphasized the Franciscans who were primarily responsible for the development of the semieremitic or hermit tradition in the order through the establishment of reforms; however, we would tragically deprive ourselves of the pure and simple heart of Franciscan eremitism if we did not consider some of the first hermits whose lives remained humble and substantially hidden in God. Many of these were among Francis's first brothers, and it is they who represent the "first fruits" of the pure Franciscan family tree. Often they were not highly orthodox in either their doctrine or their lifestyle, yet they truly burned with the mystical flame of love that so enwrapped Francis of Assisi. It would be left up to the

St. Bonaventures and the St. Bernardines of the family to bring moderate and practical reforms in order to keep the hermit and contemplative lifestyle within the Franciscan tradition; yet it is these first "foolish" followers who form the experienced root of Francis in the Franciscan tree. It is their root of simple love for the gospel poverty and prayer that has caused the Franciscan tree to bear the fruit of the Spirit and feed a hungry world for eight centuries.

Brother Giles of Assisi (d. 1262)

Brother Giles lived a life of pilgrimage, solitary contemplation, and humble service within the earliest and most famous of the Franciscan hermitages. In his passionate love for Christ, he experienced among many charismatic gifts the special gifts of rapture and ecstasy. In his asceticism, he performed manual labor, serving his brothers in building the kingdom of God on earth. In his simplicity, he became famous for his words of wisdom regarding the contemplative life, being sought after by paupers and popes as a great mystical sage. Giles must always be considered the perfect Franciscan hermit, living the Franciscan "mix" with the genius that only a simple lay brother can know.

Brother Bernard of Quintavalle (d.c. 1241–46)

After a life of activity and service, Brother Bernard retired to his beloved solitude to spend the last years of his life in pure contemplative grace. He was known to wander in the mountains above the hermitages for weeks on end, living solely from the grace of God— as brought to him through a nature unadulterated by man. Francis himself would often find Bernard rapt in prayer, deep in the woods around the first hermitages where the brothers lived. It is not surprising that the later brothers honored Francis's deathbed blessing, giving Bernard the same respect they gave to Francis as founder of the order.

John of Alverna (1259–1322)

John of Alverna spent most of his religious life in a rugged cave on an awesome and mystical mountain known as the Calvary of the Franciscan order. On this mountain John would experience the indescribable sweetness of union with Christ. Also on this mountain John would experience the "dark night of the soul" that slowly brings all aspiring contemplatives and solitaries into spiritual maturity. Finally, from this holy mountain he would venture forth with resurrected power to preach the gospel of Jesus Christ during his last few years on earth.

Jacopone da Todi (d. 1306)

The lyrical and poetical friar Jacopone Da Todi sought to live the original purity of Francis and so bring the melody of the Spirit into a world estranged by the discord of materialism. Well acquainted with the wisdom of this world's pomp and riches, Jacopone was not ashamed to make himself a fool for Christ by espousing the hidden beauty of Lady Poverty. A master of secular and frivolous lyricism, he was not ashamed to see his gift transformed by reverence for the mystical which joins the sorrowful Mother in weeping for the Crucified. After touching so many hearts with divine love, he himself was not ashamed to have his own heart broken by being imprisoned for continuing to love his friends who had fallen into doctrinal error. Finally, after writing beautiful poems and hymns about the virtues of penance and divine love, Jacopone was not ashamed to repent of his own errors in judgment before Pope Boniface VIII. After a warm welcome and homecoming by the friars, Jacopone finally died a happy and fruitful mystic while visiting a Poor Clare monastery on Christmas eve, 1306. John of Alverna is said to have miraculously appeared to minister the last rites to him, while Jacopone met Sister Death in the typical Franciscan style that so marked his life: Jacopone was singing!

10

THE POOR CLARES

⟨❧⟩

The masculine and feminine aspect of the Franciscan contemplative tradition is another dimension that must be included in any discussion of the lives of great Franciscans. This dimension is more than just the use of the words "mother" or "son" when referring to different roles within the life of the hermitage. It is lived out both in spirit and in truth by real men and real women who seek radically to follow Jesus in love and devotion. For every Francis there seems to be a Clare, who is also seeking to live the contemplative life of solitude side by side with her zealous brother in Christ. Consequently, a marvelous tradition of contemplative and solitary sisters stands equally and strongly within the overall Franciscan tradition.

Like the Franciscan brothers, this contemplative life can be found in both the original religious order of its founder (Clare in this case), or within the communities that God's Spirit has raised up within the so-called "Third Order," or more properly, the Order of the Franciscan Brothers and Sisters of Penance. Ironically, it is primarily within the Order of Penance that we find the majority of the actual "anchoresses" or hermitesses of the Franciscan family. There seems to be some debate about the authenticity of including the "cenobitic" contemplative approach of the Poor Clares within a discussion about "eremitical" approaches to Franciscanism. However, there is still much discussion regarding the original, pure ideal of St. Clare and the effect that her own religious and secular culture had on the way in which she was able, or even compelled, to live out that ideal. Some feel that Clare desired to be both more solitary in her approach to contemplative community and more free in her approach to apostolic activity, thus fitting in more authentically to both masculine and feminine dimensions of the older overall tradition of Christian eremitism. Some feel that the humble and submissive Clare was confident enough in Christ to live the life in total obedience to the authentic call that God placed on her life—and did just that! Both opinions are held by respectable "Poor Ladies" who seek to be one hundred percent true to the authentic charism of Clare.

St. Clare (1194–1253) and St. Agnes (1197–1253)

It would seem tragic if we failed to remember the lives of St. Clare and her younger sister, St. Agnes, who first went to Francis in order to follow his guidance in leading the gospel life of poverty and prayer. We must always remember the life of riches and comfort they renounced in order to be conformed to the poverty of Christ. We must remember how they had to fight boldly to live this ideal in its purity, when both parents and popes sought to turn them from their radical zeal. Also, we must remember the supernatural peace of San Damiano that was brought down like a descending cloud through the prayers of the first sisters who lived there. We should never forget that Francis himself took refuge in this little haven of spiritual peace in a hermit's shed when he was suffering from physical illness—and the affliction of the inner struggles of the order that he founded. It was during this time of refuge that Francis composed the "Canticle of the Creatures," which so powerfully speaks of the heightened awareness of the joys of this world that a heavenly life of contemplative prayer can bring. Finally, we should remember Clare's sacramental love for the Eucharist in which she boldly proclaimed Christ to those of the Islamic faith, and thus protected her sisters from the harm the conquering Moslems would have brought upon those who trusted in the cross of Jesus. While these two precious Poor Ladies of Assisi certainly stand on their own, and deserve volumes properly to cover all the edifying stories of their lives, they speak simply but surely as a pair to the concept of the Franciscan hermitage. We know that in the first years of their religious life together, the contemplative life at San Damiano certainly retained a very real semieremitic spirit of prayer. Though never pure anchoresses, the intensity of their individual prayer and the super-natural peace of their community surely reached the goal of all an-chorites and anchoresses.

Coleta of Corbie (d. 1447)

Coleta is the famous founder of the Coletine reform of the Poor Clare tradition. But Coleta began her vocation as a hermitess within the Third Order of St. Francis. After the death of her parents, she sought permission from the church authorities to have herself en-closed within a small cell next to the church. Following the example of the Benedictine nuns of Corbie, she had a window in her cell looking out onto the Blessed Sacrament. Professing the rule of the Third Order of St. Francis, she sought only to live the strict er-emitical life as an anchoress.

It was from this hermit's life that God inspired her to go forth as a reformer of the cenobitical, contemplative life of the Poor Clares. After a four-year approval, she went from convent to convent, re-establishing the spirit of prayer and poverty. In time Coleta's re-forming efforts reached to the friars, and from there out to the whole church. Beginning by finding Jesus in solitude, she was able to re-establish the spirit of prayer and poverty within communities that were devoted to contemplative prayer and apostolic poverty.

Coleta stands as a profound example of someone who first ex-perienced Jesus in solitude and privacy in order to bring spiritual renewal of even a cenobitic contemplative community. Furthermore, Coleta the Poor Clare is a witness to the fully integrated life of the Franciscan recluse who must have the freedom to answer the call to mission and reform when clearly called by the voice of God.

Blessed Beatrice da Silva (1424–91)

Beatrice represents a wide variety of inspiration to contemplative renewal within the entire Franciscan family. She also represents the integration of several religious traditions within the Franciscan expression. Beginning by living like a religious within a Dominican convent, she fits squarely within the more eremitical tradition of the penitential movement. However, seven years before her death she founded a new contemplative order of sisters who followed the Cistercian rule, giving special honor to the Immaculate Mother of God in their devotions. Pope Innocent VIII (1432–92) gave his formal approval in 1489, and a document of approval was published in 1491, only fifteen days before Beatrice died.

Three years later, Alexander VI (1431–1503) gave the rule of St. Clare to the new order of contemplative sisters and placed them under the jurisdiction of the Observant Friars Minor. Beatrice was seen as the foundress of the community that came to be known as the Conceptionist Poor Clares. In time they would make up nearly one-fifth of the Second Order, with 134 convents spread throughout Spain, Portugal, and Latin America.

At first this Franciscan affiliation seems a rather abrupt change from Dominican and Cistercian origins. However, Franciscan reform was a very real part of Beatrice's family. It seems that her brother, Blessed Amadeus of Portugal (d. 1487) became the founder of a more strict reform branch of the First Order, after spending several years within the so-called Third Order Secular. After growing as an independent reform for many years, the Amadeans were also joined with the Observant Friars Minor by Pope St. Pius V (1504–72).

Beatrice is also seen as the indirect foundress of an active Franciscan sisterhood. A Franciscan bishop convinced one convent of Conceptionist Poor Clares to devote themselves to missionary work. In 1910 the Missionary Sisters of the Immaculate Conception of the Mother of God were officially founded.

Blessed Beatrice thus represents many different Franciscan "opposites" that were successfully integrated into a symbolic whole. The Dominican and Cistercian origins represent the need for all religious traditions to work together, drawing from one another and supporting one another in their quest for spiritual growth. Both Beatrice's and Amadeus's beginnings as "seculars" represent the strong tradition of religious reform that has sprung from the Brothers and Sisters of Penance. Likewise, this brother-and-sister relationship represents the tendency toward masculine and feminine counterparts in most holistic religious reforms of the Spirit. Finally, the birthing of an active community from the contemplative womb of the Conceptionist Poor Clares represents the Spirit-led integration between contemplation and action, and the need for all apostolic activity to be born from the womb of contemplative prayer.

St. Jane of Valois (1464–1505)

St. Jane also represents a great many integrations through her life as a Franciscan. Like so many others, Jane began as both a married woman and a secular Franciscan. Her marriage to King Louis XII

(1462–1515) was quite unhappy. The king mistreated her horribly and soon gave her a bill of divorce and compelled the pope to pronounce the marriage null and void. Finding herself free of her vows, Jane decided to retire to a convent she had built with the help of twelve companions, in order more fully to live the Franciscan life. Pope Alexander VI (c. 1431–1503) approved the new institute and placed it under obedience to the minister general of the Franciscans. They took the name "Annunciates" in deference to their devotion to Mary. Their Franciscan confessor, Father Gilbert, drew up a rule and constitutions for this new contemplative community, which came to be known as a legitimate expression of the Poor Clare or Second Order tradition.

St. Jane of Valois symbolizes, again, the familial interrelationships between the First, Second, and Third Order of St. Francis. This reoccurs constantly in Franciscan history and cannot be emphasized enough, for only with this sense of "family" will Franciscans remain a relevant voice in the future. Even more interesting is the fact that this legitimate Poor Clare community did not profess the accepted Poor Clare rule. As long as some fraternal dialogue was maintained with the rest of the Franciscan family, these Poor Clares were able to profess a new rule of their own. This witness of past history has much to say to the eremitically inclined Poor Clares of the future. It means that new expressions, and perhaps even new "rules," for the Poor Clare lifestyle can be introduced into the Second Order of the future. Consequently, many Poor Clares who seek a more authentically eremitical expression can embrace the "novelty" of this more ancient contemplative traditon of eremitism by appealing to the historical precedent of St. Jane of Valois within the more recent, yet legitimate, Poor Clare past. So, by representing this general principle of introducing a new "rule" and constitutions into the Second Order, St. Jane of Valois might be able to help many sincere sisters legitimately to live a revolutionary Franciscan eremitical lifestyle while still drawing their primary spiritual inspiration from St. Clare!

By looking at the examples presented by all these sisters' lives, we can see a great many possibilities for creative integration within the Poor Clare lifestyle of the future. Far from being a religious community bogged down in the thirteenth century, the Poor Clares of today have only to draw from the living symbols of their rich past in order to proclaim boldly their revolutionary lifestyle of the gospel to the future. Consequently, today's sisters of Poor Clare have a potential of speaking profoundly to the renewal of the semieremitic lifestyle within the Franciscan hermitage of the future.

11

TERTIARIES

❧

Neither the First nor the Second Orders have most authentically lived out the eremitical life ideal of St. Francis. Most reformers within the First Order have quickly developed and sometimes degenerated into the clericalized and institutionalized form of life they were trying to change. Because of the more cenobitic, contemplative ideal of the Second Order (Poor Clares), both the solitude and the flexibility of the eremitic or semi-eremitic ideals have been hard to "fit into" the charism of the foundress, as originally envisioned by St. Clare. It was primarily up to the Order of the Brothers and Sisters of Penance to provide a home for those who were interested in living either the rule of life for hermitages, as originally envisioned by Francis, or the strict solitary life of the desert-father recluse. This seems strange since the Third Order was originally founded primarily for people living neither in the secular nor the religious state, but for married and single people wishing to live within the canonical order, or state, of penance while remaining in their own homes. Most of the celibate men wishing to live the strict eremitic religious life found the Order of Friars Minor too communally demanding and legally restrictive to enter fully into the Spirit-led solitude needed for the strict hermit. Even the semieremitic life of the Franciscan hermitage quickly came under attack and virtually disappeared during the clericalization of the order and the time of tension with the Spiritual party. As noted above, the life of the Poor Clares was, from its origin, a very definite contemplative life, but never an authentically eremitical life in either the full or even partial sense of the word. Consequently, we find a rich and abundant tradition of both the eremitic and the semi-eremitic life existing in the personal structures of the Franciscan Order of Penance after the time of St. Francis. A long list of celibate brother and sister hermits unquestionably gives the crowning glory of the eremitic ideal to the Brothers and Sisters of Penance, or the Third Order of St. Francis.

Blessed Gerard of Lunel (1270–99)

Gerard of Lunel is one of the more remembered of the penitential hermits among the members of the Franciscan family. An interesting dimension of his life is the success he had in integrating the concepts of hermit and pilgrim. It seems that after two years of the hermit life, Gerard's reputation for holiness spread. In order to escape the visiting crowds, Gerard became a wandering, itinerant pilgrim, walking on foot to the city of Rome to visit the famous churches and shrines. As a pilgrim that he found the anonymity that he desired, finally being hidden in God amidst the busy crowds of Rome. Another interesting fact is that Gerard was joined in this life of hermit-pilgrim by his brother, thus integrating the idea of both family and community with the concept of strict solitude. In all of this, the early eremitical roots of the desert fathers is authentically relived in a humble informality that clearly mirrors the life of Christ in the gospels. The fact that Gerard wore the Franciscan habit of penance from the age of five clearly includes him in the tradition of St. Francis as well.

Blessed Veridiana Attivanti (1182–1242)

Veridiana Attivanti is a perfect feminine example of the strict anchoress tradition within the Franciscan family. Building an anchorage, or hermit cell, connected to the chapel of St. Anthony in Florence, she was closed into strict seclusion by allowing herself to be walled in by her spiritual director and a large group of devoted townsfolk. She then spent the next thirty-four years in her ten by three and one-half-foot cell, the only opening being a small window into the chapel. It seems that she also cohabited the cell with two large snakes, whom she befriended by sharing her food. Apparently she did have some human visitors as well, for in 1222 St. Francis visited this holy woman to discuss the contemplative life. It was at this time that she was clothed in the Franciscan habit of penance which she wore until her death on February 1, 1242. The symbols of her life are beautiful. Seeking God in solitude, Veridiana also sought companionship with both animals and people. She sought to adore the Lord and received him constantly in the Eucharist. She also sought the counsel of a good spiritual director, including dialogue with other contemplatives, among whom Francis of Assisi most certainly belonged. Finally, the symbol of her receiving the Franciscan habit speaks profoundly to the need and the benefit of even the greatest of solitaries to belong to a supportive spiritual community within the church. Blessed Veridiana is one of the purest jewels in the crowning glory of Franciscan eremitism.

Blessed Francis Cichi of Pesaro (d. 1350)

Among the Franciscan penitential hermits who attracted followers is Francis Cichi, who founded a semieremitic community after spending several years alone. Some apostolic activity was included in this hermit's life. It seems that Francis built three hermitages after giving most of his wealth to the poor following his conversion. At each hermitage he also built a small chapel. However, at one hermitage Francis also built a hospice for poor travelers and pilgrims. After being clothed in the penitential habit of St. Francis, he devoted his life to both prayer and service. One cannot help but be reminded of the original semieremitic Camaldolese ideal of the hermitage and the hospice when hearing of this lifestyle. After disciples came, Francis of Cichi also incorporated the Franciscan custom of begging for alms in order to help support this community of hermits.

Blessed Nicholas of Forca Palena (d. 1440)

Nicholas represents both a move toward communal expressions of solitude and the inclusion of the clerical hermit within the penitential eremitism of the Franciscan family. After entering the Franciscan Brothers and Sisters of Penance, and after ordination to the diocesan priesthood, Nicholas retired from parish work to found a hermitage with several companions. He went on to found several such hermitages. Nicholas won the approval of Pope Eugene IV (c. 1383–1447), who made him director of several more convents in

Florence. Nicholas lived to a very happy old age of 100, experiencing many charismatic gifts and, more importantly, the greatest gift of all gifts—union with God.

Blessed Peter Gambracorti of Pisa (1355–1435)

Peter represents the culmination of the canonically established eremitical religious community within the Franciscan Order of Penance. Seeking only the simple life of a lone Franciscan penitent hermit, Peter's holy life of prayer and poverty on Monte Cessano converted twelve robbers who came upon his hut while hiding out in the seclusion of the mountains. Peter took the robbers in as brothers, training them in the ways of holy solitude and organizing them into a Third-Order congregation called the Poor Brothers of the Love of Christ. Retiring to the woodlands of Montebello, they lived a life of such eremitical perfection that Peter himself discouraged young, untrained men from joining their hermit colony. In 1421, Pope Martin V gave formal approbation to the Third-Order hermit congregation. Hermitages were soon founded throughout Italy until the congregation became the largest single body of Franciscan hermits. At this point other Franciscan hermit congregations were merged into the Poor Brothers of the Love of Christ. These included the popular communities of Nicholas of Forca Palena and Angelo of Corsica, Peter of Malerba, and the hermits of Monte Segestre. Long after the death of Blessed Peter in 1435, the rule of St. Augustine was adopted by the brothers and they became known as the Poor Hermits of Jerome of the Congregation of Blessed Peter of Pisa.

This community represents such a wide principle of integration that the Franciscan dimension of life is almost imperceptible when viewed superficially. The inclusion of the names of St. Augustine and St. Jerome draws heavily on the "mixed" life of contemplative solitude and communal action that so characterized them both and the communities they founded by name and deed. The merging of the various Franciscan hermit colonies into one congregation is rich with all the integrations of Franciscan eremitism, plus the symbol of the strength of a working unity that preserves diversity. The eventual canonical establishment of the hermit colony as a vowed religious community shows that while the lived religious lifestyle is always more important than the canonical status, and must always come first, the canonical status can be good if it serves to protect rather than limit authentic semieremitic life. The beginning of this colony with the conversion of robbers symbolizes the need for even the most exalted of contemplative lives always to be properly open to needs of the poorest of the poor. Yet, the screening out of weak and young brothers is a symbol of the spiritual and physical maturity necessary for those seeking the contemplative life in even a semieremitic community. Finally, the solitary beginnings of Blessed Peter Gambracorti of Pisa indicate that any large eremitical congregation should always begin with personally experienced solitude and the humble willingness never to be anything more than a lone servant of God. In this Blessed Peter joins unquestionably with the figure of St. Francis, who without thought of becoming a religious founder gave up the riches of the world simply to be a lone penitent from Assisi.

There are many other brother and sister penitents who serve as shining jewels within the glorious crown of Franciscan eremitism. There are also the venerable individuals and communities who form a more active tradition of apostolic service within the Third Order. It was the combination of these two strands of contemplative eremitic and active communal lifestyles that culminated in the establishment of the Third Order Regular of St. Francis. However, owing to the growing emphasis on the active dimension of apostolic service and the eventual clericalization of this "regularized" religious expression, the authentic eremitical life disappeared into virtual extinction and was exiled from the Franciscan Order of Penance, where once it served as a glorious crown of pure contemplative grace.

Today we should praise God that a reawakening of the Franciscan eremitism is emerging within the vowed and nonvowed religious expressions of the Franciscan Brothers and Sisters of Penance. In an attempt to rediscover fully informal eremitical roots, many contemplative communities are seeking this expression as informal "religious" who promise the three evengelical counsels of poverty, chastity, and obedience, while remaining within the so-called "Secular Franciscan Order." A strong movement in the direction of the Franciscan hermitage is reappearing in the Franciscan Order of Penance today.

Blessed Raymond Lull (1314)

Blessed Raymond Lull serves as a beautiful life with which to close this chapter of our study. An ideal exemplar of Franciscan conversion, Raymond's life is full of wholly Franciscan integrations that make him a patron of both the Franciscan hermit and the Franciscan missionary. Having received a burning call to evangelize the people of the Moslem faith through words of love rather than with the power of the sword, Raymond retired to the solitude of Mt. Ronda in order to prepare himself for his mission through contemplative prayer and scholarly study of the language, religion, and customs of the Moslem people. It was here that Raymond penned the many mystical works that mirror the contemplative heights of his life of prayer, which so spiritually empowered his philosophical works explaining our Christian faith. Seeking the support of both popes and Franciscan authorities, Raymond finally established a college in order properly to train Franciscan and Dominican friars for missionary activity among the Moslems. Raymond learned through experience how to debate humbly and innocently with Moslem scholars in such a way as to win the debate and befriend Moslem princes and philosophers. Only after several such missionary journeys was Raymond crowned as a martyr by preaching the gospel to the highly excitable lay people in the streets of a Moslem city.

Raymond Lull symbolizes the classic semieremitic integrations between solitude and community, simple wisdom and learning, vowed and nonvowed religious life, and finally, contemplation and missionary activity. His life clearly speaks to Franciscans of nearly every particular community or congregation, whether religious or lay, active or contemplative. Yet, being rooted in the prayerful and mystical experience of Mt. Ronda's solitude, Raymond remains a clear witness to the value of the eremitical life even when seen in the midst of his missionary activity. Raymond Lull thus continues to cry out as a prophetic voice from the past, calling the Franciscans of the future to be individually as well as communally centered on the mystical prayer that brings dynamic spiritual power to our every work of evangelization. Pray that we all hear his voice today!

PART II

The
Future

12

A UNIVERSAL
SERAPHIC ORDER

☙

I n his *Twenty-second Collation on the Six Days,* St. Bonaventure speaks of a "Seraphic Order" made up of both lay
persons and vowed religious, who experience the spirit's charismatic
gift of rapture in their mystical love for Jesus. He says that this "order" will not flourish unless Jesus suffers in the church, thus im-
plying that this "order" is something linked with the eschatological
events of the future, during which the church will suffer tribulation
and be fully purified. It is the "contemplative church of the future."
As he says:

> The third manner is concerned with those who attend to God by
> means of elevation, that is, through ecstasy and rapture.

> And Bonaventure said, what is this? This is the Seraphic Order.
> It seems that Francis belonged to it. And he said that he [Francis]
> was in ecstasy before even receiving the habit, and was found
> near a certain hedge. This, indeed, is the most difficult, that is,
> elevation, for the whole body is shaken, and unless there be some
> consolation of the Holy Spirit, it could not survive. And in these
> things the Church is consummated. But what this order is to be,
> or already is, it is hard to know.

> The First Order corresponds to the Thrones, the Second to the
> Cherubim, and the Third, to the Seraphim, and these are close
> to Jerusalem, and have nothing to do but fly. This order will not
> flourish, unless Christ appears and suffers in His mystical body.

Ironically, Bonaventure does not necessarily include the monks and hermits nor the friars or preachers in this "order." As a Franciscan friar, Bonaventure sometimes referred to the Friars Minor as the Seraphic Order while he was still in his youth. Toward the end of his life, however, he will speak of the Seraphic Order as something entirely mystical, transcending all organizational boundaries of the church.

It is important to note, however, that Bonaventure builds on both the monastic tradition and the centralized orders of the Franciscan friars and Dominican preachers. The monks represent the First Order, the friars and preachers represent the Second, and all lay people and religious who experience the mystical fire of the Spirit represent the Third. All three of these orders constitute the contemplative level of the church, the highest hierarchy in the mystical experience of Christ.

This indicates that there is a "new order," a "universal monasticism" unfolding in the church. Bonaventure saw St. Francis as a clear representative of this order, especially as he experienced the mystical and rapturous stigmata on Mt. Alverna. Since St. Francis was the founder of an order of itinerant friars and preachers, this order includes all Franciscans and mendicants. However, as this order is built primarily on the mystical experience of the stigmata of St. Francis, it leaps across all church structures by the power of the Spirit's wind and includes people from all orders of the church. It potentially includes vowed religious, clerics, and all the laity. It is for celibates, single and married, vowed or unvowed. It is for all who desired to be united in the mystical fire of the Spirit of Jesus Christ.

As such, the communities of this Seraphic Order must be able to include many types of people who make many kinds of commitments. It must be able to include those who seek marriage. It must also include those who seek to live as single persons without formal vows. It must include hermits, pilgrims, and monks. It must include both clergy and laity. All of these people must feel welcome in this Seraphic Order, but each must be able to make a commitment proper to their canonical state. Likewise, a commitment that unites them all, regardless of their canonical state, must be made by all.

This Seraphic Order must be open to the wind of the Holy Spirit if it is to be a true representation of the mystical experience of the stigmata of St. Francis. It must exist in the structures of the church, but it must be open to the Spirit, who also moves outside of and blows across and through the structures of the church. Openness to the Spirit must exemplify our entire way of life—openness to the Spirit in solitude and in community, openness to the Spirit during prayer and at work, openness to the Spirit in administration or in humble service. The Holy Spirit is, thus, the minister general of this Seraphic Order of St. Francis!

It is interesting to note that many Franciscan prophecies speak of a time in the future when the highly institutionalized expressions of St. Francis will lose their original fervor and zeal, and the Spirit will raise up new expressions from outside the existing structures—to rekindle the fire and zeal of St. Francis's way of life on the earth. Throughout Franciscan history this has happened time and time again, both within the tradition of the Order of Friars Minor and within what developed into the Third Order Regular and Secular.

Today is no exception to this pattern. The Spirit is raising up new expressions of Franciscanism according to the Seraphic Order of St. Francis. They are often made up of laity, yet they are manifesting the authentic charism of the founder in an exciting and powerful way. Though raised up independently from one another, they constitute a mystical "order" in the fire and zeal of the Holy Spirit. They are united in spirit and in ideals as they seek to know the rapturous fire of God, which so animated St. Francis of Assisi.

As we look to the future we need to be constantly open to the new expressions of this Seraphic Order, which in turn calls us back to our origins. We need to provide ways and channels to unite them to one another and to the existing institutions that were also once raised up by the Spirit of God.

It should not matter that they are made up of a broad cross section of people. The Spirit is teaching us that this monasticism of the future, this Seraphic Order of mystics, is made up of people from all states of life. The prophecies say that the day will come when the religious will throw off their habits and move from their poor hermitages in the woods into large houses in the cities, and that seculars will pick up their habits and move away from the materialism of the city back into the gospel poverty of the hermitages in the country. There is no doubt that this is again happening today. Let us be open to the Spirit's calling of all people to this Seraphic Order of a monasticism of the future!

13

TOWARD A NEW
FRANCISCAN EREMITISM

❧

As we seek the makings of this Seraphic Order of the future, we need to root ourselves creatively in the traditions of both the monks and the friars. In this way we might discern the work of the Spirit for the contemplatives of the future by building upon the work of the Spirit among the contemplatives of the past. Likewise, as the Seraphic Order is based on the mystical experience of St. Francis, we must now seek to understand the ways he integrated the contemplative and charismatic traditions, which helped to shape his Order of Friars Minor.

When considering the traditions that affected Francis of Assisi's initial approach to the hermitage lifestyle, and the authentically developed Franciscan eremitical traditions that have dynamically grown into our present day, we cannot help but be deeply challenged and encouraged as we presently build the Franciscan eremitism of the future. Again and again, we see the concept of creative integration touching almost every level of the hermitage life, so as to insure a maximum flexibility in living that life within the given cultures and circumstantial environments of various historical places and time. This flexible integration is never seen as destroying the rigor and discipline of the hermitage when the pristine purity of the solitary experience of the gospel of Jesus Christ remains at the very heart and center of one's visions and dreams. Only when the manmade idols of self-servitude or ego-motivated experiment in religious form expel Jesus from the center do these flexibilities in integration give way to abuses of the authentic eremitic charism of St. Francis. Even with Jesus at the center of our visions, we must still ask some very fundamental questions about the validity of many religious forms that have usually accompanied both Franciscan and non-Franciscan expressions of the semieremitic and eremitic life in Christ. We must try to untie the cultural knots that have so frequently kept the proper development of this Christ-centered life of solitary prayer bound up with unimportant externals. We must finally be still, and prayerfully quiet in God, so as to help clear the waters that have been clouded by the constant activity of the empty and lifeless traditions of men. If we approach these questions with the "mind of Christ," we cannot help but discover the truth of Jesus at the center of our eremitical dreams as we seek to live the eternal gospel of Jesus Christ without compromise within the constantly changing world of the future.

In doing this, we must remember not only that Francis was very much a man of his own time, but that we ourselves are also very much influenced by the cultural understandings and outlooks that typify our own modern Western society. We must keep in mind that while Francis of Assisi's main goal was only to live simply the gospel of Jesus Christ, he could not help but be influenced by the monastic orientation of all acceptable forms of Christian community of his day. Therefore, we must ask ourselves the even more fundamental question of whether monasticism itself is a valid expression of gospel lifestyle, or if it is just a universal, cultural carry-over from most all religions that has obscured the fresh and simple approach to living the new covenant kingdom of God as proclaimed in the good news of Jesus.

Finally, in asking ourselves these questions about the cultural entrapments of both monasticism and developed Franciscanism, we must remember that our Western culture and we ourselves are saturated with the concepts of materialism and individulism that make most all even vaguely monastic forms of Christian community highly distasteful to our self-serving and luxury-accustomed life patterns.

First, let us clearly understand that monasticism is not a form of community that has distinctly Christian origins. The monastic or semimonastic state is common to nearly every religious expression known to humankind. It is present in Jewish, Islamic, Buddhist, and Hindu expressions, just to name a few. In fact, many of the philosophers of apparently secular or pre-Christian societies grouped together in communal schools that greatly resemble the monastic state. Furthermore, when communal expressions are not evident, solitary monk-like prophets, or holy men and women, are usually found in the religious or philosophical expression of a given culture. Thus, monasticism in general seems to be a sociological phenomenon common to most all religions.

Monasticism is not something particularly unique to the good news of the kingdom of God as preached by Jesus of Nazareth, nor is it a necessary expression in radically living the gospel of Christ in an uncompromising expression of gospel community! It is true that the words of Jesus call many to a more radical expression of poverty, and some are even called by Christ to embrace a celibate lifestyle for the kingdom of God, yet we do not find either the general disciples or the particular apostles of Christ embracing a lifestyle that is necessarily monastic. Nor do we find any specific evidence of monasticism existing in the writings of the apostles or their most immediate successors. We do find a general call for all Christians to live the gospel of Jesus Christ radically and without compromise, and this sometimes even includes both celibacy and a strict sharing of material wealth. However, this communal expression always seems more general, less formal, and more fully integrated on all levels than does the uniquely monastic expression. Jesus calls all men, all women, and all children to a mysticism so profound that it is far too great to be exclusively included in the old monastic forms of the pre-Christian religions, yet it is so simple that it can be understood by the average Christian family—even the smallest child.

This does not, however, mean that the monastic communal expression is something that is improper for Christianity. It is true that Jesus brings us a covenant between God and humankind that is totally new, and as such requires us to put to death the old man and all the old ways and patterns of the world. Yet, we also know that grace often builds on nature so as to complete by the grace of the new covenant of Christ those God-given things that were beautiful, yet still incomplete, before the coming of Jesus. Monasticism is one such expression of nature that was given by the Lord and is common to most all cultures and people who sought after God as best they understood him. Thus, with the coming of Messiah, monasticism is "baptized" and completed in the truth of the new and final covenant between God the Father and man, "resurrecting" the monastic state in the full reconciliation of the cross of his son Jesus Christ, and empowering both monks and monastic communities in the full visitation of the Holy Spirit.

Nonetheless, monasticism remains a very alien concept that literally goes against the grain of almost all Western society. Though founded on theistic or deistic principles, the "American way" has become a highly self-oriented society in its approaches to individual freedom and to material wealth. True, we have exhibited a highly virtuous charity with the poor in times of abundance, and a highly global approach to common good in times of common crises, but the primacy of "self" is still very much alive in American society. This primacy of individual freedom and material wealth has led many non-American Catholics to wonder whether Catholicism works in America and also whether monasticism in general can work in such an individualistic and materialistically oriented society such as ours. Since they place such a strong emphasis on accumulating wealth, Americans find it difficult to embrace the voluntary poverty of monasticism. Since they place such a strong individualistic emphasis on personal freedom, Americans find it difficult to embrace the primacy of the common life and the necessary individual and communal obedience that serves as the structural and spiritual backbone of monastic existence. Furthermore, in a society that approaches the physical world with such economic efficiency and nonartistic utilitarianism, the sacramental and symbolic understanding of the physical realm (which is so central to both Catholic and monastic spirituality) is a truly difficult concept to grasp fully, much less embrace. For us to deny that we have been "programed" from the womb to become "good Americans" would be to deny the reality of our sociological existence. Thus, if we are typical Americans, the typical monastic expression of any religion, much less Christian monasticism, will always be a lifestyle that is very difficult for us actually to live. Oh yes, the lives of monastic saints and the monastic life in general might seem quite beautiful and spiritual when viewed from the safety of an overstuffed chair and a lifestyle of which we ourselves are in primary control. But as soon as the poverty of a monastic cell, a monastic lifestyle, and monastic obedience are actually "lived" for keeps, the American soul within us all rises to the surface and cries in rebellion against its radical crucifixion. As one writer once said, "Francis of Assisi is a very quaint and romantic saint as long as he stands down wind from us!" We should not be surprised when American monks seek to soften the "hard sayings" of the monastic tradition in the name of "revolution," and when modern youth of our culture seek out materialism and self-assertiveness, rather than the poverty and self-sacrifice of Christ as lived out by authentic Christian monks.

However, our inherent "Americanism" also can be the greatest blessing for those of us who seek to manifest a continually developing and growing monastic or eremitical spirituality and lifestyle. God not only seeks to build a totally new kingdom on the face of the earth, he also seeks to do so by transforming the existing cultures and uniting them all into a working unity that protects and amplifies the particular uniqueness of them all. God desires to bring a new work of grace, but he usually builds grace upon or through his gifts in nature. The gifts of nationality and culture are no exception to this rule. Our emphasis on individual freedom can help us to break the chains of the highly bureaucratic and overly hierarchicalized, centralized approach to both church and monasticism as we seek to return truly to the proper informal gospel roots of our particular charism as Franciscans and Christians. Our emphasis on material success and efficiency should help us to savor fully and appreciate the blessings of God as bestowed on this wealthy land, and quickly and efficiently to share our rich abundance with those who cry out in desperation and urgency for even the minimal provisions they need to survive day by day. The fact that we are a "melting pot" of all cultures should aid us in developing a truly global and fully Catholic vision regarding both monastic spirituality and an alternative Christian lifestyle in a spiritually and physically hungry world. If we use our "Americanism" as a gift from God, we might be able to bring forth a new and truly revolutionary form of monasticism that builds properly on the good traditions of the past, in order to bring the gospel of Jesus Christ as a living answer to the challenge of the future.

Yet, even with these understandings of monasticism in general, we must now ask some fundamental questions about the specific and unique expression of Franciscanism. First, let it be understood that Francis's primary goal was to break the yoke of a highly complex monasticism and to return radically to the simplicity of the unadulterated gospel of Jesus Christ. Let us make no mistake on this point: Francis sought *literally* to live the gospel of Jesus Christ. He was opposed to human interpretation, and he was opposed to rationalistic gloss. He found in most theologians and monks a lot of scholastic verbiage, but very little radical action. Francis of Assisi saw this as an abuse that had to be challenged and changed. Francis, therefore, represents a radical break with typical Benedictine monasticism, a break that would revolutionize the church and the world in which he lived. He did not seek monasticism. He sought the gospel!

Even with this uncompromising insistence of living the pure and unadulterated gospel, we still see Francis's brotherhood embracing many monastic forms. This brotherhood's concept of obedience goes beyond the gospel and enters into an understanding that is typically monastic. Unlike the apostles, the Franciscans assume a distinctive and uniform dress which, while identifying them with the poorest of the poor, also identifies them as generally religious or monastic. Unlike the informal practice of Jesus and the apostles of Jewish origin, Francis soon develops a very Western fraternity in a way that was unique from, yet similar to, monastic usages. A definite schedule complete with monastic silence is seen, not only in the hermitages, but also in the normal Franciscan houses of some provinces. So while the novelty of Franciscanism is seen in its radical break with the highly encumbered monasticism of its day, its uncompromising attitude in attempting to return to the simple gospel of Jesus did not keep it from taking on some of the typical monastic forms that so definitely affected and shaped almost every level of twelfth- and thirteenth-century Christian life.

However, we must not jump to any overly American conclusions about what Francis was really trying to do. First of all, American Christianity tends to be much less formal and ritualistic than even the simplest forms of European and Middle Eastern religion. This also holds true for the earliest forms of Christianity, which were born from the deepest womb of the Middle Eastern people. Consequently, we need to understand that we Americans tend to push toward an extremely informal approach to Christian worship and lifestyle; from a primarily cultural, rather than purely spiritual perspective, this sometimes distorts not only the real intentions of Francis of Assisi, but the original expression of the authentic church as well.

Secondly, it is safe to say that Francis was sufficiently guided by the Spirit to recognize not only the abuses of monastic and scholastic "gloss," but also the proper monastic developments of the Spirit through the church, which powerfully brought the living experience of the gospel of Jesus Christ into the culture of his day. Far from being a "fundamentalist," Francis was able to emphasize the "spirit" of the gospel before the "letter" of the law, and thus radically and literally to live the gospel in a way that was relevant to the world and culture in which he himself lived. Even when we see Francis almost irrationally insisting on the literal adherence to one isolated verse of scripture concerning the avoidance of the use of money, we must always see this "literal" adherence against the backdrop of the economic environment of an Italy in which Francis lived.

Francis's "literal approach" was therefore itself an interpreted and developed approach to living the gospel radically. Yet this approach was probably never quite consciously thought out by this seraphic Italian saint, whose primary direction was the burning flame of love within his heart fully to embrace the Crucified and thus bring all the world to salvation. For Francis, it just so happened that many typical monastic forms still helped him toward this ecstatic and charismatic mystical union.

Therefore, an eremitism of the future would do well not to rid itself so quickly of the monastic forms of the traditional Franciscan hermitage in the name of "pure" Franciscanism. Nor should we be afraid to venture into new and "novel" expressions that sincerely and authentically seek to bring a developed, informal concept of Franciscan lifestyle into the culture in which we now live. Thus, a more American version of the hermitage is totally legitimate when it is lived among Americans, just as a more Italian version of the hermitage was totally legitimate when it is lived by Italian Franciscans among Italians.

However, we should keep in mind the global dimension of our American Franciscanism before reducing ourselves too quickly into informal "houses of prayer" that are totally deplete of monastic custom. We should remember, for example, that most Buddhist monks consider the traditional Franciscan spirituality and lifestyle as the Christian religious community most closely resembling the monasticism of the orient. By the universal definition of monasticism, Franciscans are monks. Let us forget our American semantic bickerings and break free into a wider understanding that is *truly* Catholic and universally free. We are monks! Vowed or unvowed, cloistered or uncloistered—it makes no difference to the "monks" of the non-Latin Catholic Church. If we are to maintain a maximum potential for dialogue and evangelization among those of other faiths, we had best not too quickly throw off our monastic "robe" to which Francis once so zealously and devotedly clung, and through which revolutionary ecumenical dialogue and evangelization might be wondrously enhanced in the far reaches of the future. Let us embrace the truly Catholic monasticism of the future, and so come to live as revolutionary Franciscan hermits today.

14

TOWARD A
UNIVERSAL MONASTICISM

☙

I n recent years we have heard the chorus rising among Franciscans that "we are not monks." In researching early Franciscan sources we have been discovering that many of the monastic customs of the Christian West had been imposed on the friars and were in reality very much opposed to the intentions of Francis and the lifestyle of the early brotherhood. However, if we also deeply study the origins of Catholic monasticism we will discover that a truly universal understanding of the monastic traditions is much more broad and free than the limited version of monasticism that developed in the West. In comparing the studies on Franciscanism and monasticism we will find that Franciscans can rightfully say "we are not monks" when limiting the definition of monasticism to the Christian West. When expanding our definition of monasticism to its original historical meaning, we will discover that we Franciscans, who are likewise seeking to rediscover our historical origins, can much more easily call ourselves "monks."

The purpose of this chapter is to suggest a universal monasticism to which Franciscans belong. This universal monasticism was alluded to by St. Bonaventure when speaking of the Seraphic Order to which all true mystics and contemplatives belong.

Let us also look to historical origins as we consider the word "monk." Originally the monk was a hermit. The word "monk" comes from the Greek *monos*, which means "alone." The early monks did not live the lifestyle typified by the later monks of the West. These would have been considered cenobites, but not monks.

The cenobites lived in community, emphasizing the common life with brothers. They see their founder as St. Pachomious of Egypt, and their champions as St. Basil in the East and St. Benedict in the West. Of course, all trace their scriptural origins back to Acts 2 and 4, where the common life of the first church in Jerusalem is seen as a type for all communities. Most all forms of vowed religious life in the church, therefore, follow this more cenobitic pattern. But originally it would not really be considered monastic.

Originally the monks were the hermits. They saw their founder as St. Antony of Egypt and their scriptural pattern as the more apostolic poverty of Matthew 10 and 19. These scriptures proved foundational for St. Antony, as well as for the monastic reformers of the eleventh century who predated Francis of Assisi in trying to return to both the apostolic and the eremitical way of life of the early church. Francis also used these scriptures as the foundation of his gospel brotherhood and established a way of life that was at once both itinerant and eremitical. In this he is authentically a monk, even though he broke radically with the typical monastic pattern that had developed in the West.

It is also interesting to note that the "Tau" cross, so universally accepted as the Franciscan symbol, was thought of as the symbol of St. Antony of Egypt, the eremitical ideal at the time of Francis. Could it be that Francis was intentionally making a statement about a connectedness to the eremitical monastic ideal by his use of the Tau? Furthermore, much of the art depicting St. Francis uses many of the symbols of eremitism. Was this not because artists saw Francis as a Western version of the desert fathers? Not much study has been done to answer these questions definitely, but an answer in the affirmative is quite possible, if not likely.

As Jacques de Vitry said of St. Francis in his *History of the Orient:* "If we carefully consider the way of life of the early church, we discover that it is not a new rule that has been added, but rather an old one that is revived." But De Vitry also recognized the novelty of Francis in the Western church saying, "Three religious orders already exist: hermits, monks, and canons; the Lord resolved to establish these foundations on a solid basis, and so in these latter times he has added a fourth religious institution to them, the beauty of a new order, the holiness of a new rule."

In all of this we can say that Francis was really more a monk than were the monks. Yet, we must remember that he did stand in contrast to Western monasticism. In this he was not a monk. More than anything else, Francis was a man of the gospel. The eremitical and monastic considerations were secondary to the example of Jesus, and were quite probably not very paramount in Francis's mind.

Francis's original vision materialized in the founding of a community of obedient itinerants who wandered from place to place, preaching the gospel by example and word in exchange for the bare necessities of life. In this itinerant life, the brothers entered into very few of the monastic disciplines and rhythms such as the formal divine office in choir. The brothers were far too poor for such luxuries as prayer books or breviaries. Times for silence proved unnecessary and impractical for those who spent hours walking through the "grand silence" of God's flowering creation in order to reach the next village or town where Divine Providence would decide their community schedule. The friars were called to venture forth into the "cloister of the world," praying constantly and preaching whenever asked. In all of this the first friars broke radically from the stable, localized lifestyle of the Benedictine monks of the West.

Very soon, however, we see Francis establishing little "places" in the woods called hermitages. These hermitages served as refuges and retreats for the friars as they wandered the world preaching the gospel of Jesus Christ. It is in these places that we see Francis himself adamantly insisting on establishing a more monastic lifestyle. It is in the hermitage that a daily schedule is instituted, using the formal common prayers of the Roman divine office as the primary structure around which the entire rhythm of the local community would flow. This rhythm is complete with fixed times and places for silence and a "cloister," or monastic-like enclosure. We know from early sources that in these hermitages the divine office was sung and bells were rung to summon the community to prayer and common meals. In speaking of the hermitage of the Portiuncula, Francis is very clear that all of these disciplines should be observed as an example to the entire order. I suspect that many of our modern attempts to rediscover Francis's charism would seem like undisciplined college frat houses in comparison to Francis's original ideal for this holy fraternity of the church.

Even with the inclusion of these monastic customs, we know that Francis's brotherhood still differed greatly from Western monasticism. In Western monasticism, the monks were all attached to a particular monastery for life, and hundreds of monks lived together in regimented discipline. This army of obedient workers slowly built the monastery's influence and power into a position of spiritual and material "lordship" over society. Even the eremitical reforms of Western monasticism maintained many of these concepts and practices.

Francis's brothers were poor itinerant hermits who wandered from hermitage to hermitage, preaching the gospel to the entire world. The hermitage itself was a small affair, made up of only a handful of brothers. The buildings were simple and poor, as compared to the established monasteries. The Franciscans' hermitage cloister was composed of only a hedge of flowers around a small group of caves and huts where the brothers lived and prayed. Their "power" consisted of their preaching the gospel to the poor. Originally, Francis wanted the hermitages to be communities of "lesser brothers," rather than emulating the "lords" who lived within the monastic foundations of his day.

In this Francis dynamically bridges the gap between Eastern and Western monasticism. In the East, monasticism never fragmented as it developed and pluralized. Therefore, it included not only the large and powerful cenobitic model, but also that of the hermits. In the East, monks are not considered separate from one another. There are no orders or congregations. All are simply "monks," and therefore always brothers no matter which monastery one comes from. Furthermore, the concept of the "fool for Christ" and the "way of the pilgrim" continued as strong and valid expressions of obedient itinerancy in Eastern monasticism. Consequently, a monk might be both a hermit and a wandering pilgrim in the East, while in the West this would have been next to impossible for the average Benedictine monk. It is in Francis of Assisi that we see a legitimately pluralistic monastic tradition of authentic Catholicism powerfully expressed in the Christian West.

Francis himself was drawing strongly from the tradition of the "order" of penitents. It was in this group of people that we see a continual witness of both the eremitical and the pilgrim lifestyles often expressed as a rhythm from one flowing into the other. The penitents were greatly influenced by the monastic tradition of the East as Eastern monks migrated to the West to flee persecution from the Islamic Turks. Yet this "order" of penitents was not really considered monastic in the West. Although formal permission and a ceremony by a bishop or priest was necessary to enter the penitential order, the penitent was still considered as existing somewhere between the monastic and the secular states. Individuals or groups might be associated with a particular monastery, but the penitents were not formally considered monks in Western ecclesiology.

It is not at all surprising that we see Francis living as a penitent hermit at the beginning of his vocation, nor that we hear the first brothers identifying themselves simply as "penitents from Assisi" at the beginnings of the fraternity. It should seem quite logical that the life of the pilgrim-hermit continued to flourish in the Franciscan Order of Penitents from which both the religious and secular expressions of the Third Order came forth.

Thus Francis was used by God like a breath of fresh air in Western monasticism. He continued the pilgrim-hermit tradition of the order of penitents, but was somehow more charismatically empowered in his expression. The people of Italy had seen hermits and pilgrims before. They had heard the preaching of itinerant preachers. But somehow Francis of Assisi put it all together in a new way and literally shook the world.

It is also well for us to remember that Francis stands apart from even the most free expression of Eastern monasticism. Nowhere in the East do we find one individual who so completely embodies so many seeming opposites in one lifestyle. Francis exuded an unrivaled charismatic freedom. This dimension of Francis's charism is not easily defined, for it eludes articulation, but any true Franciscan is intensely aware of its reality. It is this charismatic dimension that raises Francis of Assisi above all preexisting forms of monasticism and into being the founder of an order which was something unique and new.

As we look to the future we would also do well to remember this example of fully integrated newness that Francis leaves for his brothers and sisters to emulate in their own world. We should be acutely aware of the creative integrations that are possible within all monastic expressions. We would do well to remember where we touch a common heritage with monks of both the East and West as the Spirit groans within all of us to build something creative and new as we look toward the monasticism of the future. The Franciscan spirituality and heritage has much to contribute to this universal and Catholic dialogue.

It is interesting to note that, while we do not often consider ourselves to be monks, most of the world thinks of a Franciscan when they think of monks. Some of this is the result of our own misrepresentations of ourselves, but some of this is quite authentic and legitimate. When you ask a Buddhist monk which of the Catholic orders is most like his/her own, the reply is most often "Franciscan." This is largely owing to the Buddhists' rhythmic lifestyle, which alternates between time in the monastery and time in mendicant begging. When you ask an Eastern Christian monk if Franciscans are monks, he will most assuredly reply "yes." Likewise, when you ask informed hermits and monks in even the Western tradition if Franciscans are monks, they too will often respond in the affirmative. It seems that it is we Franciscans who have problems about the word "monk." The world could care less about our own identity crises; for them we are quite simply monks.

I write this to encourage us in our rediscovery of the authentic Franciscan ideal, and to live it in a properly defined and developed way in today's world. Let us join with all of our monastic brothers as we face the challenge of the future. As St. Paul says to Timothy, "Let us not bicker about mere words," but let us hold fast to that distinct, unique, and indefinable charism from God that causes us to live the paradox of the gospel as Franciscan hermits. I pray we dig our roots deep in the soil of the past so we might reach up to new celestial heights in manifesting the Spirit-led monasticism of the future, which knows no boundaries, no limits, but unites all contemplative souls in rapturous union with Jesus Christ our Lord.

15

THE ITINERANT IDEAL

❧

"It worked in Francis's time, but it doesn't work today," is the chorus-like cry of Franciscans of our time regarding total poverty and itinerancy. We amass large sums of money and administrate large estates in the name of a poverty we say cannot really be lived.

The Franciscan hermitage of the future must break the chains of this materialistic bondage if it is to be free to be truly authentic. All of the authentic, eremitical movements of our Franciscan heritage emphasized strict poverty and itinerancy. If our present eremitical renewal is to be authentically Franciscan, we must investigate the same poverty.

The scriptures speak of two monastic patterns for gospel living: One is Acts 2 and 4 where the community shared all things in common, as with St. Pachomius and St. Benedict. The other is Matthew 10 and 19, where Jesus and the apostles were so poor that they did not even have a place to lay their heads, as with St. Antony and St. Francis. A combination of these two ideals grew out of the early church, where wandering apostles and prophets established and ministered to stable, local communities. In the writings of the early church, these two models existed side by side and complemented each other in the Holy Spirit.

The monks and hermits of the desert were poor, but they opted only for the stable pattern of Acts 2 when they established community. The general monastic pattern included monks who occasionally preached or founded monasteries, but the stable Acts 2 pattern is always seen as the model and goal for living.

With the Celtic monks of the North, we begin to see some resurgence of the itinerant ideal of Matthew 10. Many of these monks wandered to minister to the laity and built new monastic settlements throughout Ireland so that the itinerant hermit-preacher soon came to be regarded as a holy man. The concept of the pilgrim then became quite popular as monks and laymen alike begain taking vows to live their life as pilgrims in strict imitation of the Matthew 10 model of Christ and the apostles. Soon these pilgrims began to wander throughout Europe on their way to walk where Jesus actually walked in the Holy Land.

This coincided with the penitential movement that began to sweep across Europe in the tenth century. In this movement men and women would enter into the "order" of penitents. An official act of the church placed them between the status of laity or monk, investing them in the sackcloth garb of a penitent, and requiring of them a strict life of penance and prayer. Many of these people became hermits who secluded themselves in the mountains and the woods. Some also went on to become pilgrims, or itinerant hermits, who began a life of wandering from place to place in strict gospel poverty. Some began to preach, dividing their time between solitary prayer in the wilderness and apostolic action among the people of the towns and villages. Although this life proved to be problematic for the church, many great saints adopted the lifestyle as itinerant hermit-preachers.

Francis of Assisi came onto the church scene when these pilgrims were very common in Europe. As a zealous follower of Christ, Francis adapted this penitential way of life at San Damiano. Soon, he too heard the words of the gospel and literally obeyed, taking on the itinerant life of a pilgrim-hermit. It was only a matter of time before others followed him, all seeking to live the life Francis had undertaken. Instead of doing this as individuals, they did it as a united community, living in obedience to Francis and the church. The subsequent history of Franciscanism is a constant pattern of straying from and then returning to this ideal through renewal and reform.

Today, we must deal with both Acts 2 and Matthew 10 when looking at Franciscanism. I think it fair to say that most Franciscans are inspired by Francis, but they do not actually want to live like Francis. They want to be inspired by Matthew 10, but they must live according to Acts 2. They are inspired to poverty of spirit, but they must still live in the stable, religious environment of Acts 2. This is certainly Christian, and acceptable as Franciscanism, but it is not in strict imitation of Francis nor the great Franciscan reformers.

I believe the Franciscan hermitage of the future will provide an opportunity to integrate creatively the Acts 2 model of a fixed dwelling with a literal interpretation of Matthew 10. I think those who live in hermitages could venture forth in itinerant wandering from time to time. This itinerant wandering is itself a prophetic example of Jesus to a world entrapped by materialism and greed. To see friars venturing out two by two on the highways and byways, in the joy of the Spirit, to show up at a local church without a "big" advance notice to do whatever small ministry might be needed, to travel with no money, and accept no money, asking only a place to sleep and some simple food to eat—all these are ideas that would shake the parishes of this nation from their institutionalized, materialistic rut. The church of today needs the presence of such "fools for Christ."

16

COMMON PRAYER AND LITURGICAL FREEDOM

❧

By rooting ourselves deeply in the universal, monastic tradition of the past, we will come to discover what charismatic and structural freedom we have in establishing the common prayer of the future. Instead of being a kind of rigid, inflexible ritual to "perform" every day, this prayer becomes an opportunity to experience the wind of the Spirit as a united community.

We know that this moving of the Spirit was an essential dimension of the early church's prayer together. From the day of Pentecost onward, the moving of the Spirit is graphically described as a vital part of Christian prayer in common. We know that some of this prayer was very informal and spontaneous, while at other times it was very much in line with the liturgical custom of the Jewish people. Of course, Jesus himself taught the disciples how to pray, both privately and corporately, integrating spontaneous and liturgical formality even on such occasions as the institution of the holy Eucharist, or the Lord's Supper.

The early church continued this tradition by establishing certain days and times to come together and certain prayers to be prayed, yet never at the expense of stifling the Spirit or the manifestations of the charismatic gifts during the assembly. Although the church set aside certain times of the day for formal prayer, and certain days for assembly, although certain formulas were established for public prayer and certain church leaders were designated to pray those prayers, the charismatic gifts of the Spirit there permitted to operate freely through local and itinerant prophets. These apparently non-ordained prophets were allowed to pray freely in public, perhaps even to celebrate the Eucharist itself. Of course, in such matters the role of the local bishop was respected and kept strongly intact as the final authority over the assembly.

As we have seen, the early monks were primarily hermits who resided alone in caves or primitive huts or cells. Even though they often grouped in colonies, the ideal of common prayer was, at first, very foreign to their lifestyle. They spent almost all of their time in solitary work and private prayer, assembling occasionally to hear the discourse of one of their elders, or to travel to a local church to participate in the celebration of the Eucharist.

As this informal life became more popular, the solitary deserts became dotted with colonies of hermits and monks. Soon the more formal concepts of leadership and common prayer were developed. In time, rules would be written and visitors would, likewise, record their observations about the monks' liturgical practices. One such visitor was St. John Cassian, who left us the classic *Institutiones* and *Conferences*, which describe both the practices and the content of much of the hermits' common prayer and conferences.

In the beginning it seems that the monks would assemble in a common meeting room to meditate on the scriptures together. Far from being the formal monastic prayer we envision today, it amounted only to a group of rough-looking characters sitting around on the floor weaving baskets while one of their brothers read the scriptures aloud. It was primarily a common meditation service.

After a period of time the monks included the use of low benches in what they now call the oratory, or chapel. They still retained the custom of one monk reading to the assembly, but introduced the use of various prescribed postures at certain times, such as standing, sitting, bowing, or postrating themselves on the floor. This was done partially to replace the activity of basket-weaving and to keep the monks from an idleness that often brought on uncontrolled day-dreaming and even sleep. Also, the use of some common responses gradually became common for the same reason, but the monks still retained a highly meditational character in their common prayers.

About the same time, another tradition was developing in the cathedral churches. It seems the bishop would delegate the deacons to lead a common prayer service for the laity in the morning and evening within the cathedral. Since the Eucharist was still celebrated primarily on Sundays, this gave some of the laity an opportunity to gather in worship every day. This common prayer service differed greatly from the common prayer of the monks. First, the scriptures were read in a thematic cycle, whereas the monks simply read the scriptures in the order in which they appeared in the Bible. This was true especially of the psalms. Second, the psalms were sung in a way that included the participation of all those present. That was more in keeping with the original purpose of the psalm and gave rise to the art of antiphonal singing. This changed the nature of common prayer from the more meditational setting of the hermits and monks to a more participational setting in the local cathedral.

As monasticism moved from the deserts of the East to the plush cities and rural mountains and valleys of the Christian West, it also took on much of the cathedral character of common prayer. Monasteries began incorporating music and common antiphonal singing of the psalms into their worship. Soon the monasteries beame centers for liturgical experimentation, development, and reform. Gregorian chant developed in the monasteries of Europe; the rise of the monastery of Cluny and the monasteries connected with the Cluniac reform saw great experimentation in liturgical music during prayer, such as the use of polyphony and instrumental accompaniment.

The one thing the monasteries did not do was to give up their own order of praying the scriptures. Granted, many opted for a more thematic arrangement, but they did not simply conform to the cathedral customs. In the beginning each monastery would have its own method for arranging the scriptures for common prayer. With the more extended use of the Benedictine rule by the tenth century, many monasteries began using the order prescribed by that custom, yet each monastery ordained its autonomy in the specifics of many things. With the rise of the new religious orders after the eleventh century, we see entire centralized groups of communities each developing their own liturgical rite, or custom, for common prayers.

The Franciscans at first did not make much use of formal liturgical prayer, other than that common to all the laity. Since they were penitents, they undoutedly make use of repetitive prayers. Francis himself taught the friars to pray, "We adore you most holy Lord, Jesus Christ, here, and in all your churches throughout all the world, and we bless you, because by your holy cross you have redeemed the world," whenever they saw a church or a cross even at a distance. We know, too, that most of the early friars' common prayer amounted to a very free and spontaneous shared prayer, with Francis presiding as the leader of the little band of poor men. During these times great freedom was given to charismatic manifestations of the Holy Spirit.

In time, Francis also developed a great love for the divine office, or the formal common prayer for religious or monks. In the beginning the friars experimented with different forms, but finally opted for an abbreviated form which was called a "breviary." This was very compatible with the itinerant lifestyle of the friars who often found themselves praying the divine office together while traveling from place to place. The common prayer had to be compatible with the itinerant life of poverty they professed.

Some discriptions of their liturgies emerged after the friars settled down into hermitages and began opening their chapels to the public. We know that at Greccio the friars chanted, or sang, the praises of God in the presence of the people before the celebration of Mass when St. Francis reenacted the Christmas scene at Bethlehem. We know that singing the divine office was also the custom at the Portiuncula. But from the existence of the praises Francis composed and the liturgies such as the one at Greccio, we know that the Franciscans celebrated their liturgies in a way that was always creative. Francis warned, however, that Spirit-led prayer and not artistic performance should be the goal of all prayer.

The history of the Franciscan movement has always manifested a creative use of the liturgy for prayer. As the friars developed their own liturgical rite for the Eucharist and as they spread "like a carpet" across Europe, it was only a matter of time before the Catholic Church adopted many of the features of the liturgy of the Franciscans into the official Roman rite. The use of music, drama, and dance were all incorporated into "mystery plays" that attracted the attention of the street people and led them joyfully to celebrate the Eucharist in the parish church. The use of beautiful music, colorful banners, and brilliant church art brought life to the community celebrations of faith in the church and prepared the fallow ground of the human heart to receive the seed of the preaching of the word of God. Throughout history the Franciscans have retained the joyful and free availability to the Spirit that so animated St. Francis and the early friars during common prayer.

Today, this means we have much freedom as we build a common prayer practice for the seraphic community of St. Francis. We must remain obedient and respectful of church structures for prayer because they guide us during prayer, but we have much freedom and flexibility within both our own heritage and our own structure.

We should always strive to maintain an attitude and environment for deep prayer and meditation during common prayer. We should never so rush through prayers that we do not have time individually to reflect and meditate on the scriptures. In praying the psalms we should be open to many forms. We could pray them antiphonally, giving each side the opportunity to participate and listen to the words of the psalm. We could also use new music to accompany prayer, praise, and worship where appropriate. Ideally, the psalms should be sung, but the recitation of the office without music is certainly a part of our tradition.

We also have great freedom as far as the content of the common prayers is concerned. As Franciscans, we have a great love for the divine office, but as a continuing manifestation of the universal monastic and eremitical tradition, we should feel free to use our own order for praying the psalms. With proper approval and community consent, some incorporations of the early monastic and eremitical practices might prove an aid in heightening the experience of prayer and meditation during the divine office. The special composed prayers of St. Francis and his friars also give us a precedent for adding special meetings and devotions outside of the divine office or Mass.

Of course, our entire Franciscan heritage of charismatic freedom and spontaneity should also be manifested during prayer. We would do well to remember the charismatic gifts manifested during those times of common prayer before the early fraternity could afford liturgical books, and we might do well even to lay aside our liturgical "possessions" from time to time to relive that spontaneous prayer of the first friars. Within even formal liturgy, times not only for individual reflections, but for individual sharing of charismatic gifts with the group should still be allowed. Spontaneous praise in word and song should not be excluded from our use of formal praise with the psalms. The Spirit is to be given freedom in our praises. Shared "homilies" or reflections on scripture readings are often a way really to share our faith with one another and to hear the "prophetic" voice of the Spirit coming through the voice of the community. Likewise, much freedom and time should be allowed after the formal intercessions, so that we might really share in the intercessory ministry of Jesus, who is our great high priest.

Throughout our common prayers, opportunities should be provided for individuals in the community to share their artistic gifts. Music, drama, and dance can all be tastefully incorporated into the common prayers of the community.

Of course, throughout it is important that our common prayers never become "performances" or lose their simplicity. The role of the prayer leader should always be respected, and reverence before God should never be minimized. In all, any freedom during liturgical prayer should be used only to lead us into prayerful union with God. Freedom used as a cloak for our artistic pride or ecclesiastical rebelliousness is sin. The common prayer of the Franciscan hermitage should ever remain humble, obedient, and poor. Otherwise, we have strayed from the path to God.

17

INTEGRATING EAST
AND WEST

❧

A s the Seraphic Order of the Spirit unites all monastic and
lay traditions of the church, so does it unite the East and
the West. We know that the first hermits and monks were from the
Christian East. As monasticism moved West, however, adaptations
were made to the culture of the West. Today, as we bring this universal monasticism into the modern culture of the West, we will
need to root ourselves ever more firmly in the soil of the original
monasticism of the Christian East.

This can happen on many levels. The "classic pattern" of integration between solitude and community in the hermitage will become apparent even in its geographical layout which consists of a
"*skete*" or *laura* with a cluster of huts or cells around a common
chapel, work, and dining facilities. As the ideals of poverty and itinerancy permeate the hermitage, so will the hermitages remain
humble and poor, never becoming too attached to overwhelming
structures like those of some monastic empires. The need for some
presence in the poor inner cities will qualify, or amend, this pattern
to include a *kellion*, or monastic cottage, where all live under one
roof. The latter will take on more of the nature of a house of prayer.
Both the *skete* and house-of-prayer patterns are explicitly mentioned
in the Carmelite rule. That rule in itself does much to blend the
East and the West into a working and flexible whole.

Much has been said throughout this book about the Franciscan
integrations in governmental structures, communal commitments,

common prayer, and other related topics. Most pre-Franciscan reform communities of the West that influenced Francis were intentionally trying to integrate the monastic practices of the East within
the Western church, and this fact says much about the need for authentic Franciscans today to continue in the spirit of this creative
mix. The mix will be, however, not so much a calculated integration
of similar ideals as an ecstatic and rapturous union in the fire of the
Holy Spirit.

On the spiritual level, Francis's repeated prayer, "My God and
my All," has much in common with the "Jesus Prayer" of the Hesy-
chastic tradition of the East. Our constant "breathing into" this
prayer should open us to a constant prayer in the Spirit, or divine
breath of God. Much creative experimentation in this area could be
tried in the hermitages of the Seraphic Order of the future. Francis's
emphasis on the role of the Holy Spirit as minister general of the
entire order places us in union with the teaching of the Russian
Orthodox St. Seraphim of Serov, who stressed the experience of the
Holy Spirit as the peak of our whole Christian life. Bonaventure
speaks of the experience of being "on fire" for God in a way similar
to the mystics of the East, who speak of God as both fire and light.
St. Bonaventure also speaks of the "knowledge of unknowing" in
union with the divine fire at the end of his *Journey of the Mind to
God*. This allusion to a divine darkness places him squarely in the
tradition of the Eastern mystics. Likewise, at the end of his *Triple
Way*, Bonaventure speaks of the way of "negation," which places
him on a par with the Eastern Christian mystics who speak of "apo-
phatic" knowledge, or that which can be expressed only by stating
what it is not.

I have alluded elsewhere to the Franciscan similarities with at
least some of the external dimensions of Buddhist monasticism. The
Buddhist monks live a life of rhythm between meditation and action,
alternating between time in the monastery and time in mendicant
wandering or pilgrimage. The presence of their daily begging has
much to say to Franciscans who shy away from such a radical following of St. Francis in today's world. The Buddhists' frequent pilgrimages in walks for peace and social justice have much to say to
those of us who are so entrapped in the "big-is-better" ministry
pattern that we have forgotten the small, humble beginnings of St.
Francis and the validity of a simple yet radical ministry of presence.
Finally, the Buddhist practice of making temporary commitments
to live as a monk for part of life and as a family man for another
part of life, has much to say to our sometimes inflexible structures

that hinder rather than aid the working of God's grace through us unto all the world.

A very creative integration between our tradition as penitents and "nature lovers" can also be achieved with the Far Eastern religions' practice of Hatha Yoga. This Yoga is simply a physical exercise that is conducive to meditation. Contrary to what some think, this can be "baptized" in Christ and used to glorify Jesus as it helps us both to pray and to be good stewards of the "temple of the Holy Spirit" all at the same time.

As we come from a tradition of harsh bodily penances that actually can harm our bodies, we would do well incarnationally to "touch" the crucifield and risen Jesus through a bodily discipline that actually helps our bodies while primarily aiding our prayer. The practice would also build on our Franciscan tradition that sees the Creator praised and glorified through all creation. Likewise, the use of breath prayer can integrate both the Christian East and West with the meditation technique of our non-Christian brother-monks.

It should be pointed out however, that while we can share much in the physical or psychological experiences of non-Christian monks, the ideal behind our lifestyles, prayers, and practices remains very different and is sometimes even radically opposed to those experienced. For us, a personal relationship with Jesus remains the Alpha and the Omega of our life. For a non-Christian this is not necessarily so.

Eastern religions do not center on the Jesus of Christianity. For us as Christians, the center of our meditation and contemplation is Jesus. For the Eastern religions it is "nothingness," nonpersonal spirit, or personified expressions of deity other than Jesus. While the Christain might rightly recognize the grace of God at work in these other religions, for us they remain only partial expressions of the fullness of truth. For us the absolute fullness is found in Jesus. Often the ideals of Eastern religions might be in actual conflict with the basics of Christianity: i.e., a personal God as contrasted with a nonpersonal divine "energy"; a full doctrine of grace as contrasted with a doctrine of reincarnational achievments; and the fullness of God as revealed once and for all in Jesus Christ, contrasted with Jesus being but one of many partial or full incarnations. We might share many experiences in common with Eastern non-Christian mystics, i.e., the nothingness of passive contemplation, certain bodily and mental responses during times of meditation and contemplation. But for the Christian these things all flow from centering only on the person of Jesus rather than on the phenomenon or technique itself. Certainly, some techniques might be good tools in meditation and prayer, but they are only tools. Jesus remains the beginning, the end, and the center of all mystical experience for the Christian. It is Jesus alone who leads us fully and safely to the Father in the power of the Spirit. Any other way can lead to very real spiritual danger for the non-Christian, and for the Christian it is not only unnecessary but intolerable.

Various forms of Eastern Yoga deal with very real spiritual and human powers. Both mantras (the chanting of a particular deity's name or sound) and Yoga postures are intentionally connected to a particular spirit or god for the true Eastern devotee. These spirits are not some harmless "psychological" reality. They are real. From a Christian perspective they are not all good spirits, and any direct invocation of them through mantra or posture is foolish dabbling in idolatry and demonism.

On a more human level, it is certainly true that there are latent energy powers within the human soul. These forces are extremely powerful. They can theoretically be used either for good or for evil, for healing or for destruction. They are also quite mysterious. Yoga links most of this power to gods, spirits, or even demons. Only limited research has been done regarding these powers on a scientific level, and even less from an intentional Christian perspective. For the inexperienced it can be dangerous ground. It is like nuclear power. In and of itself it can be used for good or evil. But its dangerous nature and our limited knowledge make its safe use questionable, even with the best of motives. The same holds true for the powers stirred up by Yoga. They are real and should be handled with caution and care.

Despite all this I do believe some integration with Yoga is possible for the Christian. But it then becomes Christian Yoga. It must be totally baptized and made new, keeping what is pure and true, and completely putting to death that which is born from the author of lies. Pure light always comes from God; it is only the devil and deceived human perceptions that color its purity with darker hues. If we can separate the pure light from the erroneous colorations, we are all right. Theoretically and theologically I believe we can in Christ. Pastorally, I believe we limited human beings must be quite careful.

On both a spiritual and energy-flow level all that is accomplished through Yoga's techniques is already accomplished through Spirit-filled Christian prayer. The redirection of life forces so scrupulously sought after in Yoga happens spontaneously, almost unconsciously, through pentecostal prayer in the Spirit and full operation of the charismatic gifts. One has only to point out the "pure aura" of the Christian so often seen by those who see or photograph auras, or the transmission of "heat" through the hands of the charismatic healer. In all this the effect is accomplished by centering on Jesus rather than on a technique or the effect itself. The main difference is that in Yoga it is accomplished by an intentional technique, and in charismatic prayer it is accomplished solely through God's grace. In charismatic prayer we leave the dangerous dabbling in the psychic, trusting in our own human power. This is not to say that such creative adventure and discovery cannot be done by a Christian who recognizes Jesus as the giver of all truth and knowledge. It is only to say that charismatic prayer usually accomplishes the same and much more without the risk of spiritual deception and error. We do well to remember the solemn warnings of the desert fathers and the scriptures about angels of darkness who come as angels of light to deceive many.

The purely physical aspect of Yoga, however, is easily integratable into the Christian experience. In this we simply keep the body healthy through prayerful exercise and diet out of respect for the human body as the temple of the Holy Spirit. We can also engage in an ecologically sensitive and reverent attention to all our bodily needs out of respect for the creature who bears the traces of God, and is also the object of the redemption accomplished through Christ. This should not really be something new. It is the result of age-old Christian beliefs and theology. It results in our whole life becoming a reverent prayer.

All in all, as we venture more and more into the mystical life and experience of this Seraphic Order of St. Francis, spoken of by St. Bonaventure, we see many opportunities for East-West integrations. They have many structural ramifications in our hermit colonies and communities, but they deal most primarily with the mystical experiences of the heart. Likewise, they have a positive effect on the meditation practices of both body and soul. Here we have but touched on a few possibilities for investigation. It would take an entire lifetime and many books fully to reach and discuss proper conclusions.

18

OBEDIENCE

There is a crisis in the church today concerning the whole concept of obedience. For centuries the church built up a highly legal concept of obedience. In this scheme of things both the "superior" and the "subject" operated on a very impersonal level, with both the command and the obedience being seen as a matter strictly defined by canon law and community constitutions. Through it all there was the faith that this rather impersonal approach to faith built one's personal relationship with God. While there certainly was merit in this kind of thinking, it tended to move contrary to the more authentic understanding of original eremitism and monasticism, and actually produced a minimal understanding of a living and personal faith-filled obedience.

In early eremitism and monasticism obedience was a very personal matter between a discipline and his spiritual master. There were no rules. There were no constitutions. There was no canon law. But ironically, a level of obedience developed and persisted that would be almost unthinkable between the superiors of today's communities and their members. I believe this is because it was more personal and less legal. Disciples sought out spiritual directors to help guide them along the way. These directors, or abbes, had to be experienced in the way of Christ before others would be drawn to them. It was because of their holiness that others could unhesitantly place themselves under their direction in almost blind obedience. Consequently, the levels of obedience were much higher in the informal, personal approach of early eremitical monasticism than what we have witnessed in the more formal and legal approach of recent centuries in the West.

Nevertheless, the obedience of even early monasticism remains very difficult for most of us. Let us now look at some of the reasons why. It must be understood that most of the scriptures support a more nonmonastic approach to obedience. This means that an individual Christian is, in fact, called to abandon self-will totally to the will of God. This is done by the individual existentially seeking to hear the Spirit's wind-like voice through prayer and then objectively testing the word of the Spirit with the Word of God, as found in scripture, and as discerned and interpreted through the Spirit-led laity and the apostolic leadership of the church. While the incarnational leadership of the church is involved in this obedience, usually that which is called for by the church is quite general and logical in helping an individual to follow the way of our master, Jesus of Nazareth. The example of Jesus and the law of love are primary in this, leaving much to individual discretion in Christ, with only occasional input by the leadership of the church.

A monastic approach to obedience includes all that is involved in the nonmonastic approach, but continues into a more particularly intense understanding of a spiritual leader's involvement in an individual's growth in his/her death to self-will. Likewise, while the example of Jesus Christ and the logic of the law of love remain the primary standard of this approach, many times a blind abandon to the will of God working through the spiritual leader is involved. In this approach, the wish or command of the spiritual leader might seem quite unnecessary or illogical to the disciple-monk.

While we see this kind of blind faith asked for between human beings and God, or between the disciples and Jesus in both the Old and the New Testaments, rarely is this approach to obedience found in the biblical accounts of the relationship between a human spiritual leader and a disciple. We see the apostles definitely guiding their disciples in the general areas of faith and morals, but rarely does the New Testament give evidence of a monastic approach to obedience between them. The reference to a leader as a "shepherd," when Jesus is seen as the primary "good shepherd," is the closest to seeing Christ himself in our community leaders. Nowhere do we find the apostles exercising unconditional authority over the details of a person's life. The closest thing would be the story of Ananias and Sapphira in Acts 5. It is true that the community of Acts 2 and 4 "shared all things common" and submitted to the apostle's authority, but even this seems to have been entirely voluntary. So the story of Ananias and Sapphira primarily involves disobedience to the Spirit working through the apostles.

However, this does not invalidate monastic obedience. As with monasticism in general, we can say that it is not necessary to living the radical gospel life, but we cannot say that it is not compatible with that life either! As monasticism itself was "Christianized" with the coming of Christ, so too was the monastic concept of obedience, which was and is present in every known form of monasticism in the world.

Furthermore, this approach to obedience was present between Jesus and his disciples, so it is not at all surprising that we find the radical abandonment of one's self-will into the hands of a "spiritual father" in the early history of the Christian church. If this blind faith was necessary for the spiritual growth of Jesus' disciples, it is not un-Christian for the legitimate spiritual leaders of the monastic community to use this same method for the very men with whom they have the responsibility to help conform to the image of Christ.

Vatican II also speaks not just of religious obedience but of all the evangelical counsels as a more intense, and therefore demanding, expression of the gospel commitments expected of all baptized Christians. The *Decree on the Renewal of Religious Life* says, "They have handed their entire lives to God's service in an act of special consecration which is deeply rooted in their baptismal consecration and which provides an ampler manifestation of it." Chapter VI of the *Dogmatic Constitution on the Church* says that such a profession brings "more abundant fruit from this baptismal grace. . . . Thus he is more intimately consecrated . . . by virtue of firmer and steadier bonds," and "serves as a better symbol of the unbreakable link between Christ and His Spouse, the church." The commitment required by Christ of all believers is good. The commitment required by Christ of religious and monks is more intense and better.

We now seem to have two major approaches to scriptural obedience. The first involves an absolute and total obedience to God, with an incarnational obedience to the leaders of the believing community in areas of basic faith, morality, and the practical realities of community life. This way involves a very real death to self that definitely helps conform an individual to the image of Jesus Christ, who "learned obedience through what he suffered." Submitting oneself to the "yardstick" or canon of scripture is challenging enough when discerning one's own spiritual growth in Christ; it is much more so when submitting oneself to the input of a spiritual leader of the faith community for an outside, objective opinion of one's progress. Let no one be fooled: This way can provide ample opportunities for sharing in the suffering of Jesus.

The second way, however, goes beyond the first more obviously scriptutal way. It involves submitting oneself to the nearly absolute guidance of a spiritual father or mother in both the internal and external affairs of one's spiritual life in comunity. While most of these areas will be, like the first way, dealing with basic areas of faith, morality, and the practical affairs of living in the faith community, some of the areas will involve the testing of one's total death to self by commanding things that are humbling, or even at first glance illogical. These latter areas are nearly impossible for the average American Christian to bear, but he/she who passes through such tests will come out like fire-tried gold!

In this second way, the role of the spiritual fathers or mothers and their relationship with their disciple-children cannot be overemphasized. In this approach the spiritual fathers/mothers definitely become an active symbol of Christ to their respective community. This means that the faith-filled disciple will look beyond the obvious human frailities and sins of their spiritual father/mother and see Jesus himself directing him or her individually and communally through such leadership. It also indicates that a very real and profound love relationship of parent and child must be developed in Christ. The child must trust totally by faith that Jesus will direct him or her through the spiritual father/mother. In order for this to work in God's perfect plan, the spiritual fathers/mothers must love their disciple-children even as Jesus loves them and makes them disciples. An authority that involves the gentle strength and personal concern of the Good Shepherd must be primary in the spiritual shepherd, who is called to lay down his life with Christ for his sheep. Thus, the love relationship between the spiritual parent and child becomes a supernatural reality that defies the logic of words and enters into the mystical realm of God's love.

It must be understood that Francis of Assisi definitely followed the monastic way of obedience and spiritual fatherhood and motherhood. He undeniably fought against the abuses and corruptions of the monastic systems of his own day, but he also continued to embrace the traditional monastic understandings of obedience and spiritual parenthood as very real ways to follow the gospel of Jesus Christ in simplicity and humble zeal.

In this we can see Francis fulfilling the role of spiritual father in a way very similar to the early desert fathers. Francis dealt with his sons with the love of a caring father, even using the term "mother" to emphasize the gentleness and tenderness that should be present in the leader who is called to symbolize the tender Jesus to a community. Yet like Jesus, we also see "the little poor man" rise up in manful strength and righteous anger in order to correct abuses within his gospel community which was to be ever mindful of the strength and the just wrath of the heavenly Father. This is all very similar to the desert *abbe* who personally guided his spiritual sons with both the love and the strength of God.

Francis also follows the way of the desert fathers in testing the faith behind the obedience of his sons, sometimes requiring an obedience that was personal, immediate, and seemingly blind. In this, both Francis and the desert fathers are very similar to the approach of the Zen masters. We can see this in the classical story of Francis requiring one of his sons to plant cabbages upside down, or in Celano's description of Francis requiring a son not just to seek to follow the commands of a superior, but even to seek to fulfill the thoughts and wishes of a superior before they were spoken. This approach is a definite return to the early understanding of the monastic "abbot" who is to be given an obedience that is both personal and absolute—within certain limitations.

There is of course the danger of abusing this kind of obedient relationship between a disciple and a master. This would involve, for example, the ego-destruction practiced by many Eastern masters with their devotees and disciples. It has also been practiced by superiors toward their subjects in Christian monastic and religious communities. In this practice a person is supposed to learn a total death to self through a series of humiliations and tests inflicted by a superior. While this approach might be somewhat justified in some cases, in most cases it involves a cruelty that goes against the practice of love in gospel relationships. Death to self, yes. Obedience, yes. Cruelty, most assuredly, no.

The gospel does not destroy a person's ego or sense of self-identity. It simply takes the ego off the throne in a person's soul which only God can occupy. Ego-destruction will kill a person. The ego must only be put in its proper place. This is the role of the sensitive spiritual director or superior: to help a person be what he or she is truly called to be in Christ. Most of the time this involves encouragement and support. Only rarely does it involve correction, and even less the humility that can only be accomplished by humiliation. This practice of imposed humiliation rarely does any real good to the one needing humility, and generally places the soul of the superior or minister in jeopardy when carrying out a judgment usually reserved to God alone. Praise God, the law of the church and the constitutions of our communities require a leadership that cannot easily exercise such harsh extremes.

We should also catch the spirit and letter of Vatican II if our approach is to be fully Franciscan. Francis himself sought to conform his whole gospel lifestyle according to the teaching of the church councils of his day. If we are to be authentically Franciscan, we must do the same with the church councils of our day. The councils are different, but the Franciscan attitude remains the same.

According to the *Decree on the Appropriate Renewal of Religious Life*, monastic or religious obedience "will not diminish the dignity of the human person, but will rather lead it to maturity in consequence of that enlarged freedom which belongs to the sons of God." This applies to the profession of the "evangelical counsels" in general. Chapter VI says, "Profession of the evangelical counsels, though entailing the renunciation of certain values which undoubtedly merit high esteem, does not detract from a genuine development of the human person. Rather by its very nature it is most beneficial to that development. For the counsels . . . contribute greatly to the purification of heart and spiritual liberty."

Of course, the success of such an end depends upon the mutual openness of both superior and subject to the Spirit of God. As the *Decree on Renewal of Religious Life* also states, "Each superior should himself be docile to God's will in the exercise of his office. Let him use his authority in a spirit of service for the brothers." As to human development, it continues, "Governing his subjects as God's own sons, and with regard for their human personality, a superior will make it easier for them to gladly obey."

Canon law also dictates a similar balanced approach to obedience. Canon 601 states that superiors "act in the place of God," but they must "give commands that are in accordance with each institute's own constitutions." Furthermore, "The authority which superiors receive from God through the ministry of the church is to be exercised by them in a spirit of service. . . . By their reverence for the human person, they are to listen willingly to their subjects and foster their cooperation for the good of the institute and the church, without prejudice, however, to their authority to decide and to command what is to be done." Thus, the superior operates with real authority from God and actually stands in God's place in the community. But this is not without very real conditions that check and balance all tendencies to an autocratic demand for a subject's obedience.

I would like to point out that, as a leader of my particular community, I rarely make decisions on my own. Nine times out of ten community decisions are made by consensus or democratic vote. Only if I perceive the direction of the community to be in direct opposition to the founding vision will I step in to veto with my authority as superior. This, however, is done only in obvious and extreme circumstances. I can count on my fingers the times I have found it necessary to do this. This option, of course, is contingent upon the maturity of the members. The better the discernment of the community regarding candidates, the better the quality of the members. This enables me to release a great amount of responsibility into their hands, precisely because I can generally trust their own spiritual maturity and discernment abilities. All is done with respectful dialogue whenever possible. Only in rare cases of urgent necessity do I decide something "on the spot," and this is usually in small, more domestic affairs. If I don't trust my community enough to listen to what the Spirit is saying through them, then they will not trust the work of the Spirit in me. It is a two-way street. If either superior or members do not walk in this spiritual trust, the process eventually breaks down. Ultimately, it is faith in God that makes this process of obedience and submission work. It is the Spirit who works through both the superior and the members of a community. Without faith the whole thing becomes a vain exercise in human psychology and bureaucracy.

I would also point out that while Francis was definite in his return to the purity of the ancient monastic ideal of obedience, he also extended the ideal through a radical concept of humility and tenderness for the superior. Not only was the superior a spiritual father, he was also called to the tenderness of a mother as well. Not only was he a parent, he was also called to be a little brother, an example of the perfect Friar Minor. He was not to be a superior by human standards; he was to be a servant and a minister. The friars were to be able to talk to the minister, even as an employer would talk with his employee. The minister was thus the employee, or servant, of the entire fraternity. He was called not so much to command, but to listen and act in Christ. This cut right to the heart of the prevailing abuse of religious authority in Francis's day.

This humility and spiritual authority seem quite unacceptable to many, if not most, of the religious Franciscans of today's Western culture. We have come to a more modern understanding of personal responsibility before God and the role of obedience within our communities. Thus, Franciscans have often opted for the nonmonastic model of spiritual leadership and obedience within their communities.

Our leaders exercise a very limited authority that is checked and counterchecked with community councils that exist on local, provincial, and international levels. Furthermore, the leaders can be easily voted out of office after a very short time if their spiritual authority begins to threaten our oftentimes cultural, individual independence. Ironically, there is sometimes a shortage of real spiritual humility in these leaders, for they see themselves more as administrators than as spiritual pastors.

This approach to leadership, however, picks up on the dimension of Francis's understanding that sees the brotherhood as the primary authority and individual, spiritual freedom and growth as a vitally necessary dimension to the gospel community. It also safeguards the community from the tyrannical leadership of power-hungry "abbots" who seldom exercise their leadership with the spiritual sensitivity of the early monastic *abbe,* who patterned his authority on the personal authority of the gentle strength of Jesus.

The same approach has also caused some very real problems that coincide with the problems of Western society. The lack of the lifelong personal love commitment between the *abbe* and the son has caused many modern Franciscans to swallow entirely the "do-your-own-thing" illusion of a collapsing Western society. While it might look good to the cultural eye and taste sweet on the tongue, we could find that this attempt to introduce a mock obedience and an undisciplined individualism into Franciscan religious life quickly becoming the hook that could pull our entire spiritual body out of the life-giving waters of our earlier observances. With this modern model we have often copied the utilitarian mindset that sees our leaders as mere administrative functionaries, or at best capitalistic, commercial visionaries, leading a community of individualistic, undisciplined spiritual opportunists.

It should be remembered that Francis attempted to keep his itinerant hermit-preachers from wandering outside of obedience. The "do-your-own-thing" approach of many such wandering monks has been one of the classical curses of monastic life in both the East and the West. Francis tried to establish a community that would provide for the life of the wandering pilgrim, while still retaining the obedience and discipline of the hermit-monk.

In the beginning Francis himself served as the spiritual father who lovingly governed his spiritual sons who dwelt in the cloister of the world. The primitive concept of the desert-father "abbot" remained the same, but the geographical boundaries of the monastery expanded to the farthest ends of the world in fulfillment of Jesus' great commission. The brothers were free to be blown by the wind of the Spirit across the face of the earth, but always in obedience not only to the general direction of the church, but also in particular submission to Francis as the classical spiritual father of the community.

Eventually the local *custos* became necessary, and it was only with Francis's prolonged illness that a successor, or minister general, became a reality in the community. From the wording of the rule, it is evident that Francis saw the minister general as his true successor and full spiritual father of the order. So the original desert-father concept developed yet substantially stayed the same in Francis's mind. Furthermore, it seems that this successor was to be in office until death, in a way similar to the monastic tradition of the desert, which saw the relationship between the *abbe* and the son as a permanent, lifelong commitment of love. Only if this successor proved to be obviously unacceptable was he to be replaced by the valid election of another brother of the community. All of this is very much in line with the classical monastic tradition of the abbot and the community. Only the geographic boundaries of the cloister were changed.

However, we know from subsequent Franciscan history that once Francis stepped down from the minister-general position, real trouble began to stir. The reign of Brother Elias brought a mixed blessing to the order, which made the new community very wary of the unchecked authority of the "successors to St. Francis." We know that in a very short time the role of the minister general shifted from the traditional monastic concept of the contemplative spiritual father to the more administrative-servant role of the temporary leader of a democratic, active community. This developed for very real and valid reasons, but the development nonetheless indicates a major shift from the traditional monastic concept, not only as regards the geographic cloister, but also in governmental and spiritual leadership. Given the problems of today's individualistic and noncontemplative Western society, these hierarical developments need to be clearly understood, defined, and properly checked if the Franciscan community is to remain a powerful spiritual and contemplative force in the West.

In the Franciscan hermitage of the future, this means a radical return to the concept of the humble spiritual father or mother and the disciple child. In a society where commitment is cheap and transient from place to place and from family to family, we need to reestablish the stabilizing concepts of love relationships in Christ that will bring forth obedience and a vitalized spiritual family— faithful to speak of God's permanence to this unstable and passing world.

This can happen by simply reawakening the traditional Franciscan values of obedience and family within existing community structures. Instead of seeing the superior as a mere administrator, we can see him or her as a true spiritual parent who ministers as Christ to brothers and sisters—just as a parent would lovingly minister to a child. A real humility and example of service by the minister will keep him or her always approachable and always revered. This is a simple but very real way radically to return to our contemplative roots, while still recognizing and working within the developed, active structures of our respective Franciscan communities.

We can also more radically return to primitive Franciscanism by establishing substantially permanent spiritual fathers and mothers within the new Franciscan hermitages that are cropping up around the world. These spiritual parents might or might not be in the formal leadership role in the hermitage. In this a very real integration between the primitive First Order tradition and the more monastic Second Order tradition can be seen; it also indicates a more complete integration with the wider eremitical tradition of the East and the West, which was so prevalent in the tradition of the eremitical colonies of Franciscan penitents, and thus provides a more general, and less particular, orientation toward the growth of a movement in the future.

In either pattern a simple return to the eremitical way of Francis should be primary. In Francis's *Rule for Hermits,* the concept of spiritual mother and son places the Franciscan hermitage squarely in the tradition of the desert fathers, where the abbot was a loving spiritual and temporal guide to his sons in Christ. Francis's insistence on the primacy of the brotherhood, as mothers and sons exchange roles periodically, guarded against the abuses of the power-hungry monastic abbot of the time. Coupled with Francis's original experience and primitive ideal for the spiritual father of the entire itinerant hermit community scattered throughout the "cloister of the world," we can see that the true and original monastic concept of abbot was very much a part of Francis's way of following the gospel of Jesus Christ without compromise. Based on this personal and spiritual concept of leadership, Francis expected a form of obedience by the "son" that is unquestionably monastic. It was only the untimely illness of Francis and the unfortunate abuses within the new community that caused the order to deviate from this original experience and dream. If we can return to a freedom that is disciplined, and a mendicant wandering that is humble and obedient, then we can speak prophetically to a world languishing in pseudo-individualism and in a freedom that is false.

19

A QUESTION OF LEADERSHIP

❦

The question of leadership within the Franciscan hermitage is a bit of an enigma. Francis spoke little of leadership in the hermitage, so the question might seem to some to be both inappropriate and necessary at the same time.

Francis left us a "rule" for hermits that is informal at best, not even mentioning any formal minister within the hermitage. The "leadership" of the hermitage was a very charismatic affair, involving the concept of service rather than authority. All authority was left to the *custos,* or local minister, who was to visit the hermitage periodically.

We know that the concept of leadership and spiritual fatherhood was not at all lacking from the lived experience of Francis and his friars. Francis fits squarely into the tradition of the desert father or the Russian *staretz.* Brother Giles, too, is often described in similar terms during his pilgrim-hermit career, even though he never is spoken of in any major leadership role in the order. Finally, some concept of "guardian" or local minister existed in the places we know were hermitages, even though the rule never mentions such a role. We can only assume that many times the official ministers were also seen as true charismatic leaders who could easily be described as spiritual fathers.

We should also examine the role of the Franciscan spiritual father as seen against the backdrop of the religious climate of Francis's day. Since Francis saw himself as spiritual father of the entire order, and the minister general as his legitimate successor, we would do well to study and compare the role of the minister general with the monastic abbot to discover the similarities and differences that make the Franciscan heritage both historically credible and charismatically unique.

When Francis of Assisi established his order of little brothers, he broke radically from the more fragmented monastic pattern of the West. In many ways he did this by simply reforming the abuses in the monastic life of his day with a constant insistence on a return to gospel poverty and fervent prayer. He also did this by extending the limits of his new community's cloister to the ends of the earth. By extending the concept of cloister, he centralized the whole community under one common superior who acted as the spiritual father of the entire brotherhood. He did not establish a network or federation of independent or autonomous monasteries, each with its own abbot. Other ministers developed on provincial and local levels as the community grew, but one of the novel dimensions of the Franciscan Order continued in the concept of the one common superior.

In the beginning this one common superior, or minister general, was seen as a spiritual father who was to guard and shepherd his family of brothers for the rest of his life. Obviously, Francis filled this role in the beginning, being seen as the spiritual father of the entire movement. As a father remains the father of his children all his life, so too did Francis write in the rule of 1223 that the minister general was to remain in office as a spiritual father until his death. The minister general was to be a permanent superior.

As the great Franciscan scholar Cajetan Esser said, "Francis is 'pater' (father) in the full spiritual meaning of the world. . . . The position of the superior resembled that of the individual monasteries of older orders; nevertheless, the office and its exercise were permeated with and inspired by the particular spirit of the new brotherhood."

It is important to see that in this Francis did not break with the monastic pattern, for the monastic pattern was based on the apostolic pattern as depicted in the scriptures. It is very clear that the earliest monks of the East and the West saw their abbots as lay spiritual fathers, who governed their communities in much the same way as the apostles and the bishops governed their churches. Just as the monastery was seen as a quasi-church, so too was the abbot seen as a quasi-bishop. Francis broke with monasticism by extending the cloister to the world, but he did not break with monasticism in the establishment of the minister general, who was to be like a spiritual father, or abbot, for this novel monastery that stretched throughout the world. Thus, Francis established this gospel community squarely in the apostolic tradition of the scriptures.

This was part of Francis's ideals until he himself resigned from the office of minister general because of ill health and his sickness of heart over developments and abuses within his own order. Peter Catanii succeeded Francis but died shortly after his election. Brother Elias succeeded Peter temporarily until John Paventi was elected. John Paventi could not take the tensions of this new community, so he also resigned. Elias again was elected, but he proved to be so much of a dictator that the brothers appealed to the pope who removed him from office. Albert of Pisa was elected as his successor. He took the first steps to give the community some control over the minister general in case he acted more like a dictatorial abbot than like a true spiritual father. It was only a matter of time before the minister generalship became a temporary office, often better suited for an elected administrator than for a charismatic spiritual father. The minister general has remained a temporary leader to this day among all four orders of Franciscan friars.

It is interesting to note a parallel tension in the Benedictine tradition. Like the Franciscans, they too felt the need to control their abbots when the latter abused their authority. Following the lead of the mendicant orders like the Franciscans, the Benedictines tried the idea of temporary abbots. This worked well in many respects, but it was not consistent with early monastic history, nor did it demand the mutual responsibility and obedience of working out the family relationships between a spiritual father-abbot and his spiritual sons. Today, many monastic communities are returning to the original concept of a permanent abbot. However, they have developed and rediscovered ways in which the community retains a strong voice in the government of the monastery.

It is well to note that most all institutions which had a permanent leader also gave strong power to the chapter or council of brothers. Among the Carthusians, for example, the prior general of the entire order is required to offer his resignation once a year to the local priors gathered in general council. They either accept or reject this resignation based on the prior general's performance, and can either keep him in office for life or replace him after one year. A similar arrangement was established in all monastic and mendicant orders of the West. The minister, prior, or abbot generals were permanent responsibilities, yet the proper council could always remove the brother from the office. In Franciscan spirituality, the minister on any level is always supposed to be willing and ready to step out of leadership if so required.

We Franciscans would do well to follow the Benedictine lead in trying authentically to return to our own roots in this matter. True, willingness to step down from leadership should be present in all of our leaders, including the minister general. Likewise, experience has proven that the community must maintain valid controls over the abuses of authority possible with an overly authoritarian minister general. We need to rediscover the concept of the minister general as a true spiritual father, whose office by that definition must be a lifetime responsibility.

This raises the whole question of committed family relationships. Both the wider monastic and the Franciscan traditions speak of their communities as "families" who are lovingly led by spiritual "fathers" and/or "mothers." Just as the relationship between the brothers and sisters of a family are ideally permanent, so too should the relationship between the parent and the child be permanent. At different stages in our lives these roles may be substantially changed, but the parent remains the parent and the child remains the child. Any developed relationship between them always flows from this primary reality. All of this requires loving responsibility and a commitment to see relationships through, even when it seems humanly impossible. The result is growth on the part of both the parent and the child, and a stability within the family unit that benefits every person involved.

The same holds true for religious families. Too often the lack of a permanent spiritual father or mother has undercut the stability of an entire community and has cheated all its members of rich opportunities for spiritual growth. The roles of spiritual parent and child are charismatic realities that are permament if instilled by the Spirit who gives us all a share in God's love. It is this love responsibility that makes the whole thing work. Without this understanding it all fails and crumbles.

Of course, this early monastic and Franciscan tradition of permanent general superiors must be seen against current canon law regarding most religious communities. Canon 624:1 states: "Superiors are to be constituted for a certain and appropriate period of time unless constitutions establish otherwise for the supreme Moderator and for Superiors of an autonomous house."

A full understanding of the above helps us to discern our true uniqueness in the overall Christian eremitical tradition. By seeing the similarities between the original idea of a minister general as permanent spiritual father, and the similar pure ideal of the monastic abbot we can discern that Francis was not opposed to monastic tradition in this area. By understanding that Francis extended the limits of the cloister to include the whole world, we can visualize a radically different concept of eremitism emerging from Francis's heart than had previously existed in even the eremitical reforms of the monasticism of the West.

For Francis the hermitage was a solitary place of prayer for a larger order of itinerant wanderers. It existed not as an isolated, independent community with its own abbot, but as a transient community cooperating with the larger community of itinerant preachers. At first the hermitages were places that served as centers from which the brothers would go forth to preach. While some brothers stayed in one hermitage for many years, others might go from hermitage to hermitage as they traveled from region to region to spread the gospel of Jesus Christ. After the friars established other "places" and "convents" in the cities and universities, the hermitages added to their character the dimension of retreat from places of active apostolate. In all this the hermitage was seen as a part of a larger community that was itself governed by a spiritual father, or minister general, with the help of provincial and local ministries.

It is interesting to note that only after the tensions between the way of life in the city convent and the way of life in the hermitages seemed too great that the need arose for the hermitages to develop their own government. Even when this occurred, the hermit friars did not opt for the more monastic pattern of a permanent spiritual father in each hermitage. They chose to continue to incorporate the hermit life with the itinerant wanderers' life, thus necessitating the continuance of the concept of the vicar or minister general as spiritual father of the entire community. This is seen in all the Observant and Capuchin reforms.

The development of the order as penitents presents a somewhat different perspective. The hermit tradition within the Order of Penitents grew from a less-centralized organization. It seems that many independent founders were raised up by the Spirit to live the eremitical life. Only after they attracted followers did they feel a need to come together as a centralized order directly under a minister general. When they did this they affiliated, not only the hermits but also the more active communities as well. Thus, a similar organization to the First Order developed in what came to be called the Third Order Regular, but because it developed from independent founders and groups, the autonomy of each community has been an important part of their tradition.

This autonomy is further accentuated when considering the independent communities that have grouped together not as a centralized "order," but as federations of autonomous congregations. True, very few eremitical expressions exist today within these federated congregations, but the contemplative expression of Franciscan monasticism is not at all lacking. Thus, the concept of an independent hermitage under the care of a lifetime spiritual father would not be at all illegitimate within the federated tertiary tradition. A federation of these autonomous hermitages might prove to be very advantageous, both to the communities and to the eremitical movement within the Franciscan family. Furthermore, it might be this tradition that most authentically fits into the desert-father tradition, which might have the most to offer to mutual dialogue and support among all eremitical communities of the Catholic faith.

As we look to the future we can discern several legitimate approaches to leadership within the Franciscan eremitical movement. The firist would involve a hermitage existing in union with the province, which exists under the overall fatherhood of the minister general of the entire order. This would be in keeping with Francis's original idea that there should not necessarily be even a local superior in the hermitage, but that all formal leadership comes from the larger order. This would work for any branch of the First Order, the Third Order Regular, or any larger Third Order congregation. A second approval would involve these hermitages existing under the direct authority of the minister general, either individually or as a group. This would follow Francis's idea for the hermitage of the Portiuncula and would follow the examples of the original Observant and Capuchin reforms. In this arrangement each hermitage is more apt to have a local minister, and the entire group is more apt to become its own custody, province, or even its own independent order with its own minister general. Finally, the idea of forming either a new federation of independent, eremitical communities, or of forming a new congregation of Franciscan hermits is also very possible. All of this gives the freedom to develop creatively without having to put "new wine into old wineskins."

These ideas all involve formal and canonical steps of governing the Franciscan eremitical movement. But it seems to me that there remains a more informal way that would help unite all Franciscan hermitages in a manner that would be very true to the spirit of Francis's original "rule" for hermits. This way involves establishing an informal "covenant association" of Franciscan hermits. It would not be an attempt to form a new order, but would rather be a way to unite all Franciscan hermits of all Franciscan orders informally and with minimal structure. The commitment of a covenant could be made but never with the intention of more than a commitment to love and support one another as we live out the eremitical life as Franciscans. The government of such an association would involve only a few people to coordinate and organize the "chapters" or "conferences" and perhaps some information center. The idea of obedience and discipline would be left primarily up to the existing formal Franciscan communities to which the hermits would canonically belong.

The "spiritual fatherhood" of this movement would then be left up to the individual communities and the wind of the Spirit blowing through various charismatic individuals within the movement. It would greatly respect and express in a modern, developed way, Francis's informal hermitage structure which did not even provide for internal government or local ministers. It could prove to be very exciting.

20

THE HABIT

~

Directly related to the concept of obedience to God and to a spiritual *abbe* is the sign of consecration known to-day as "the habit." As monasticism itself is under critical questioning by many religious today, so too is the value of a distinct religious habit.

The habit is the traditional clothing worn by the monk and extends back to the very origins of monasticism itself. Being clothed with the habit was the incarnational symbol of one entering the monastic state under a spiritual father. This was especially true in the early eremitical colonies before the development of public vows. It should be clearly understood that in days long before official religious vows, the habit was the sign and symbol of what would later become known as the evangelical counsels of poverty, chastity, and obedience. In this sense, it could be argued that the importance of the habit is actually greater than the public vows, in that the habit is a sign of obedience that was developed prior to religious vows.

It is true, however, that what actually constituted the habit is seen to be very flexible in early tradition. Usually just a poor and simple garb represented one's renouncement of the pomp and pride of "the world." We see early on that this garb was distinct from the dress of nonmonks, yet was definitely affected by both local culture and climate.

In style the habit ranged from the fairly complex and symbolic garb described by John Cassian to the crude garment of skins worn by St. Antony of the Desert. Many of the nuns of the desert wore a hood rather than a veil, as did many of the nuns of Celtic monasticism. Yet, the veil grew out of the penitential tradition in which a woman's hair was shorn and her head totally covered. Over the years both the East and West adapted and developed monastic dress to both climate and culture; however, a distinctly monastic garb has always persisted within the traditional and orthodox mainstream of the working of the Spirit in the church called "monasticism."

In scripture there is no direct mention of Jesus wearing any kind of special garment. We know that the incarnation of the Word among men was done specifically to consecrate the ordinary or mundane, and to make the lowly the highly exalted as a manifestation of God's glory on earth. From this it might be argued that Jesus was as the prophet says: "There was in him no stately bearing to make us look at him, nor appearance that would attract us to him."

Jesus was also a Jew, and a Jew who was consecrated from birth to the service of Yahweh. He was also of the more orthodox expression of Judaism. This means that he did conform to some of the external signs of his consecration and of his faith. Uncut hair and beard, plus the long, floor-length prayer shawl of his day were probably distinctive signs of Jesus' religious position and faith to the people among whom he lived.

Francis of Assisi was a man who sought to follow Jesus without compromise. He was also a man who stood squarely within the reform tradition of Christian monasticism, radically returning to the concepts of the founding fathers, while looking forward with a revolutionary vision that was constantly developing fresh and new expressions.

We know that Francis of Assisi willingly adapted a garb that was traditionally monastic as well as novel in its return to gospel simplicity. His "monastic garb" consisted of a simple floor-length sackcloth tunic cut in the form of a cross, with a hood and trousers. He also exchanged his leather belt for a piece of rope and removed the shoes from his feet. We also know that the garb of the "lesser brothers" was distinct from the secular garb of the people, and constituted a recognizable identity as a religious whose habit was a sign and symbol of his consecrated life—both to himself and to the world. Thus the Franciscan habit became a universally recognized religious or monastic garb of a community of brothers and sisters who lived in the simplicity of the gospel.

As Esser says, "That the Friars Minor constituted a true brotherhood was made apparent externally by their uniform attire." Esser also says, "One must not, of course, imagine it as a habit in the present day sense, that is, one deliberately chosen and agreed upon beforehand. But from the very beginning the members of the brotherhood were marked externally by their clothing." This was probably owing to the extreme poverty that so radically associated them with the poor of the world. But the habit was clearly religious or monastic. Esser continues, "We would not be mistaken in seeing in this religious habit a powerful bond of union in the new fraternity, by which it was held together and united as it spread throughout the world. If thereby the friars aligned themselves with the age old tradition of Christian monasticism, such a situation became generally accepted them."

The *New Fioretti* includes a story from *Verba Conradi* which is a prophecy of St. Francis concerning the habit. "The time is at hand when a friar will throw off his habit or tunic in the road and return to the world. And a worldling shall pick them up and go with them into the desert." We see this fulfilled in many of the new eremitical Franciscan communities today.

Today many experiments with the habit have been tried with both lesser and greater degrees of succes. Many communities have tried discarding their habits completely, while others have retained them for use only during the liturgy. Some have zealously returned to wearing the long habit constantly, while others have instituted the concept of an adapted habit or cowled shirt.

The first two approaches are certainly taken by good, healthy Franciscan communities, but it must be understood that these approaches are not fully consistent with either monastic or Franciscan traditions, or with authentic understanding of the purpose of a religious habit. Granted a time without the habit is phychologically healthy in order to establish an authentic self-image in Christ, as well as to minister as a normal person among the normal people of society. But part of a Franciscan's self-image in Christ in his monastic or religious call from God, and today's world is crying clearly for a visible witness of a holy and exciting lifestyle—distinct from the drudgery of daily life. The habit acts as an incarnational sign and symbol of God's call, which leads us on to something new and fresh in Christ.

Furthermore, the habit is not seen as a liturgical vestment in traditional Franciscanism or monasticism. The habit is symbolic, but it is to be the normal day-to-day garb of the monk. This symbolizes the consecration and holiness of even the most insignificant and mundane part of the monk's life. Wearing a habit only for community liturgies might be good in at least keeping some idea of the habit alive in religious communities; however, it should not be thought that this is a fully Franciscan approach to the purpose of a religious garb. The Franciscan habit should be simple and plain enough to be worn during almost all daily work, but it should be enough of a sign and symbol of the consecrated life that it can be proudly worn during the most solemn of liturgical celebrations.

The second two approaches are more traditional but still have some problems. The wearing of the "cowled or work shirt" and pants effects a monastic and Franciscan symbol that is both practical and culturally relevent to modern dress, but even this adapted habit is unusual or unique enough so that it usually creates more questions than does the traditional long garb which is universally recognized throughout the world as the "Franciscan habit." The long brown Franciscan habit is easily identifiable to the public in general; however, it is a very impractical garb for much of the work of the modern Franciscan hermit. Ironically, it is the new Franciscan semieremitic communities that are involved in active and public ministry who have returned to the constant use of the long habit. They have found the public response to be very positive, as they visibly symbolize the incarnational presence of a holy God in the midst of a world struggling to be free from sin. It is the more strictly eremitical communities who are more exclusively wearing the cowled shirt and pants. This is perhaps owing to their being substantially free of public opinion regarding their call to a hidden ministry in Christ. Both of these latter approaches see the validity of some form of the monastic habit as a symbolic garb to be worn as daily clothing, rather than mainly as a liturgical vestment.

The popular understanding of the habit by the public should be taken into account, especially when the Franciscan witness and presence among the people is so much a part of our tradition. By and large, the public understands the visual statement of the long, brown Franciscan habit, or a sister with some sort of veil. The traditional habit speaks of radical commitment and mysticism for which both the old and the young hunger. The modified habit, or cowled shirt, is good but is often too much like secular dress to indicate that it stands for anything at all. Our sisters were once asked if they were a Brownie troup when as a group they wore their work shirts in public!

Both the hierarchy and the laity would like to see religious wear their habits, but the religious themselves often find them intolerable. I believe this might be because of the psychological images that the traditional habit still brings to mind for the older religious who experienced religious life before Vatican II. For them the habit represents an entire way of life that was overly externalized and artificial. For the young the habit might represent a challenging, spiritual alternative to the materialism of the modern world, but for the older brothers and sisters it still represents archaic religious institutionalism. Their problem is understandable, and I agree wholeheartedly with their protest against a cold, lifeless religion that had degenerated into institutionalism and legal form.

When all has been said, all four of these approaches have a positive content that should not be overlooked. It is important to maintain the concept of sign and symbol in liturgical worship. It is important to relate to the public with signs and symbols that are easily recognizable and generally accepted. It is important to use signs and symbols that are both practical and culturally relevant.

Most communities that are adapting a combination of the latter two approaches are finding they fulfill the positive contributions of all four approaches. The cowled shirt and pants, or work habit, is both distinct from yet similar to the average informal dress of the modern world. The long Franciscan habit is both universally recognized as the robe of the celibate monk and is obviously fitting for liturgical worship. Furthermore, even the long Franciscan habit is a garb simple enough in which to perform many, if not most, of the tasks faced by the Franciscan hermits.

Another dimension of the monastic garb beyond incarnation and symbol is the call to the cross of Jesus. It was no accident that Francis cut his first habit into the shape of a cross! The monastic garb is designed to be practical, but it is also designed to be penitential. It is not supposed to be the soft, luxurious garment of those who keep company in the palaces of the kings and princes of the world. It is supposed to be the rough penitential garb of one who practices repentance by facing life in the self-sacrificing austerity and solitude of the desert. As our concepts of penance mature from the sometimes imbalanced excesses of the Middle Ages and return to a more biblical balance and interior view, surely our view of a penitential garb will mature. The call to penance and the call to the cross should always be symbolized and experienced in the true habit of the Franciscan penitent or the hermit-monk. As we are called to discipline the passions of the flesh and the desires of the world, we will find the rough garb of the hermit to be a constant sacramental of God in helping to remind us and aid us to this end of penance.

The concept of the habit is also significant in light of the recent phenomenon where lay people, both celibate and married, desire to wear some kind of simple garment to symbolize their radical gospel call. In this the celibates will often opt for the traditional long habit, while the married folk will opt for a cowled shirt, or adapted habit. This phenomenon is especially important in light of the prophecy which shows the seculars picking up the habits the religious cast off, then going out again to inhabit the hermitages the religious have abandoned. According to the prophecy, new forms of Franciscan and religious life will be raised up by the Spirit, independent of the prompting of the church. Such is the case with many of the new communities of lay hermits, who again wear the habit today.

One of the final dimensions of the habit is the concept of integration between East and West. As we integrate all past monastic spiritualities into a new and creative whole in Christ, the habit should symbolize such a creative development. A simple return to the habit of the past is not a true symbol of today's spirituality in Christ. It is with this in mind that the combination of the adapted habit, or the cowled shirt and pants, and the long, brown monastic robe is very fitting. They symbolize both the old and the new, the East and the West, the penitential and the practical. Yet in all this, the element of incarnational sign and symbol, which is essential to the call, is retained.

Many of the problems concerning the habit *are* problems only because they reflect an identity crisis among many monks and religious in today's church. Uncertain about even the fundamentals of monastic or religious life, they are even more uncertain about wearing a strange garb from a strange religious culture, which supposedly symbolizes something they neither understand nor support. This is an honest position and one that needs even further attention by the church in the years to come. Yet, when persons have a strong, interior call to live as monks within a Franciscan hermitage, the external sign of the habit never seems to be that much of an issue. They seek their own self-image only within the incarnational image of Christ crucified that God calls them to through their monastic call. Called by their divine Lover to this monastic life, they easily conform to the legitimate image of this call on earth. Romantic? Yes, it is! For it involves the mystical love of God which in turn involves the heart. It is only when the heart is involved that even self-sacrifice and crucifixion seem sweet. Those who seek to solve problems with only their mind and a view of protecting their own self-image have problems with such an approach to religious life.

However, those who see this love as the root and foundation of their whole life find it much easier to be at peace about such external dimensions of monasticism as the religious habit.

Some may think it a shame to have to spend so much time and energy on the external clothing to be worn in the Franciscan hermitage of the future. However, the habit remains a symbol of the interior spirituality that motivates the community or colony of hermits. Deeper spiritual matters, such as obedience, penance, integration, and incarnation are all symbolized by the "habit issue." Such matters remain at the very heart of traditional Christian monasticism and Franciscanism eremitism, and must be clearly understood and embraced before any balanced attempts can be made as a revolutionary expression in the future.

21

VOWS AND PROMISES

❦

Let us briefly discuss the whole concept of communal commitment, for much of Franciscan life hinges on the pivotal concept of communal commitment. We have already discussed this commitment taking the form of vows or covenant promises within the new monastic communities of the future and have also briefly touched on the subject in our early summary of the life of the desert fathers.

Francis was interested in literally following the gospels. A brief overview of scripture would be a good place to begin a further explanation of the subject.

It should first be understood that monasticism as such is not explicitly mentioned in the New Testament, nor is the concept of monastic vows found anywhere in scripture. However, it is true that the general concept of vows is found in the Old Testament. Also, a more particular concept is found in the "Nazarite vow," which called an individual to live a life set apart unto God through both personal asceticism and public symbol. This nearly "monastic" vow is witnessed in the lives of the prophets and judges: Samuel, Elijah, and of course, Samson. There is even strong evidence that John the Baptist and Jesus were Nazarites in that they were, like Samuel, consecrated unto the Lord from birth by their parents. However, neither the Nazarite nor the general vow of the Old Testament was really "monastic," in that no formal "communal" commitment was apparently involved.

Furthermore, the ecclesiastical involvement of a priest was minimal, leaving especially the profession or pronouncement of the
vows a very private matter. It is interesting to note that while the
New Testament is even more silent on the subject of any Christian
form of vows, St. Paul does take a very short Nazarite vow in Jerusalem in order to prove his Jewish orthodoxy to the Judaizers.
Beyond this the closest thing to "monastic vows" in the New Testament is witnessed by the voluntary sharing of goods by both celibate and married members of the first Christian community at Jerusalem. Even as the Christian community grew, it seems that
baptism itself served as a serious enough commitment for any dedicated Christian to make, making any further form of commitment
superfluous to the radical gospel life that was required of every
Christian.

Only when the zeal and seriousness of the overall Christian community cooled did the further ascetical and monastic forms of life
appear. At first, only isolated and scattered individuals responded
to the call of God seriously and radically to live the words of the
gospels. However, these holy men and women soon attracted disciples and grouped together into informal ascetical and monastic
colonies. The practical complications of having many disciples necessitated some formal structure and some formal commitment as
these informal colonies soon developed into formal communities.
Thus the Christian concept of a further "vow" was born for the baptized Christian who now wished radically to live the gospel life.

What actually constituted this vow was sometimes quite vague.
In the beginning it seems that a mere change of dress into the ascetic, penitential garb was symbol enough to assume that the disciple would be obedient to the elder of the community. To this day
the Coptic monks in Egypt take no monastic vows and profess no
written rule, living the rule and commitment of "love" just as did
the desert fathers before them. Later, however, the mention of actual
vows is made by the concils of the church, yet what constituted
those vows remains very unclear. Only with the *Rule of the Master*
and the *Rule of St. Benedict* do we hear of a formal ceremony ac-
companying the pronouncement of a monastic vow. Furthermore,
only by the time of Pope Innocent III do we see the concept of
public religious vows necessitating the particular vows of poverty,
chastity, and obedience. From that point onward, a very legal attitude prevailed regarding what constituted a public religious vow
and a private vow, taken by penitents or seculars. Consequently,
the lines between the monastic or religious state, the penitential

state, and the secular state became much more defined and much more ecclesiastically controlled by the bishops and popes of the church. This development became truly necessary owing to the abuses against monastic vows, the private commitments of the penitential state of life, and the private vows made by lay people. Yet as we look to the legalities of all these developments, we cannot help but be somewhat saddened by the loss of the simplicity and fully integrated flexibilities of both the first Christians and the first communal expressions of ascetics and monks.

It was into this complicated religious environment that Francis of Assisi surfaced when trying to live simply the gospel of Jesus Christ. Seeking also to be fully obedient to Jesus and his church, Francis willingly embraced and fit into the necessary structures and forms that served to protect the integrity of the legitimate religious expressions of his day. The solemn profession of an accepted rule of life and formal religious vows were some of these structures and forms necessary for the survival of Francis's little community within the highly hierarchicalized Catholic Church of Pope Innocent III.

To the present day this highly legal approach to vows has continued. The Roman Catholic Church has developed many neat legal categories into which all communities are placed if they are to survive. Unfortunately these different categories often greatly separate the communities and make serious dynamic integrations among them virtually impossible. Consequently, vows to a particular community often overly particularize the brothers' or sisters' personal vocation and overly fragmentize the overall monastic community of the church. This is true especially of the "mixed" semieremitic life of the Franciscan hermitage, which seeks to integrate so many seemingly opposites into a working whole. It is interesting that in the Christian East these categories are much less restrictive. One simply becomes a monk of a monastery and flows from the contemplative to the active life, according to the rhythm of the Spirit in the community. Nonetheless, the list of problems and complaints concerning the highly legal approach to monastic vows in the West is much too long to consider fully here.

Two fundamental questions must be asked when considering the commitments of the Franciscan eremitism of the future. First: Is the concept of the publicly vowed life an essential dimension of the authentic Franciscan eremitic life? Second: What forms of commitment are possible for this Franciscan religious life in the future?

In response to the first question, it should be understood that Francis of Assisi definitely embraced Pope Innocent III's whole structure for religious life. True, Francis did not initially set out to become a monk or religious. In the beginning, Francis's fraternity itself was but a loose-knit, informal brotherhood of penitents who sought radically to follow Francis in living the gospel of Jesus Christ. However, shortly after these informal, charismatic beginnings, Francis seeks to establish formally the new community with Pope Innocent III in order to protect the starry-eyed group of spiritual dreamers from the threat of internal abuse. Francis willingly placed himself and his fraternity under the very real legal restrictions of the religious forms of the Roman Catholic Church. Francis saw these restrictions as good protections for the internal purity of his ideal.

It was the church that later would more or less force Francis to compromise, or moderate, his ideal in order that it be more practically lived out by a great multitude of followers. Yet, even here Francis obeyed the church, for the church did not prohibit those who sought to live the rule more radically from doing so. Francis in no way saw the concepts of formal religious life and formal public vows as destroying the authenticity or the zeal of his attempt to live the gospel of Jesus Christ in total simplicity and without compromise.

We can assume that Francis did not approach this question with the cool detachment of an objective canon lawyer. Francis burned from within with a highly existential fire of love that longed fully to embrace the Crucified with every fiber of his being. If the formal, religious life of the thirteenth century could help him toward this end, then Francis would ardently embrace it as embracing the Lord himself. If it kept him from the Crucified, then he undoubtedly would have fled from its reach as from the devil himself. As it stood, the religious life of the church helped Francis and his fraternity in objectively organizing itself and in subjectively putting to death the "self-will" of a fallen world that so shuns the cross of Christ.

It is difficult to say whether the formal religious vows and structure are necessarily an integral part of the authentic charism of the Franciscan hermitage. If one seeks a more informal form of the Franciscan hermitage that does not include the more monastic understanding of commitment to a community, formal religious vows might prove to be much too burdensome and restrictive. Something less binding or permanent in character would be more suitable for such an expression. However, we should insist on this only if we are establishing a twentieth-century Franciscan hermitage that is seeking total freedom from the monastic customs that Francis so willingly accepted in thirteenth-century Italy. Therefore, we should seek purposefully not to be true to Francis's literal, external expression of Franciscan lifestyle in order, hopefully, more authentically to discover his internal intention of pure gospel lifestyle, as lived within our modern world. This approach is experimental but is certainly not invalid.

As to other possible forms of Franciscan commitment, the religious vow certainly always has been and will continue to be a legitimate and authentic expression within the Franciscan hermitage. This applies to both pontifical and diocesan communities. It applies also to temporary and to permanent vows. Unquestionably, the religious vow is proper for those Franciscan hermits or hermitages that exist within an established religious community. Undoubtedly, many new Franciscan eremitical communities will seek to be properly established as new religious congregations. It is an established fact of traditional Franciscan commitment.

However, it is the concept of covenant promise that has the highest potential for bringing a renewal of the eremitic expression to the "entire" Franciscan family, and a form of radical gospel commitment to all the people of the new Seraphic Order. There are many reasons for saying this. More flexible than vows, and more particular and intense than the normal secular Franciscan profession, the covenant promise has potential for being a legitimate religious expression that properly crosses the canonical lines of individual Franciscan communities. Thus, Franciscan covenant communities might properly include members from many different formal religious communities or orders, not only bringing the recognized commitment needed for the stability of the new Franciscan hermitages, but also bringing a renewal of the eremitical lifestyle into the older Franciscan communities. Eventually, an entire association of these Franciscan covenant hermitages could form an informal network of mutual support that could help renew the entire Franciscan family. This could become an informal way of realizing the Seraphic Order that crosses all canonical boundaries, yet calls us all to a particularly intense life in the Spirit.

The covenant promise could also serve to aid those who seek a more narrowly or exclusively American expression that is substantially free of the monastic and religious dimension of early Franciscanism. The covenant promise can be serious enough to give the needed commitment to an informal contemplative house or colony that seeks to become an intentional community. But it can be informal enough to be ratified or dispensed by a mutual discernment between the individual and a community that sees the universal

principle of Francis's radical return to gospel poverty as more primary than the thirteenth-century formal religious expressions.
Whether or not one feels led by God to this more informal type of
expression, one cannot help but recognize its legitmacy as an authentic experiment of the greater contemplative Franciscan family.

The commitment of the proposed covenant promise might be
either temporary or permanent. The *temporary covenant* would be
ideal for a member of a formal religious community who seeks to
join a Franciscan covenant hermitage and then return to his or her
own religious community after a few years. This commitment is
also ideal for the more informal house of prayer that sees changing
membership as a flexible arrangement which serves as a visible,
modern expression of the gospel mendicancy for which Francis
fought so desperately in thirteenth-century Italy. It could also serve
as a temporary monastic training ground and a prayerful discernment
place for those who seek a permanent religious or secular vocation
elsewhere. Thus, temporary covenants could serve a wide variety
of religious and secular Franciscans who seek to live temporarily
in an authentic hermitage of the Franciscan tradition.

The *permanent covenant* commitment might serve for either religious or secular Franciscans who seek always to live the religious
life in the hermitage. For the formal religious, this would necessitate
an approval that would allow them to remain in the covenant hermitage yet truly retain a canonical tie with their formal religious
community, which could be quite healthy for all parties. For the
"secular," this commitment could be considered as morally binding
as a formal religious vow, for it is this "religious" covenant promise
that often most authentically resembles the early monastic vow; it
might also involve a commitment regarding poverty, for instance,
that might be more compatible with their secular calls. Thus, entire
quasi-religious communities of hermits who profess permanent
covenant promises and/or public vows can arise. Of course, these
permanent commitments would be preceded by a series of temporary commitments in a way similar to the use of temporary vows
before the profession of permanent vows.

It bears repeating that in the beginning the monastic commitment
was not anything as formal as a religious vow, nor is anything like
a modern religious vow found in the early church of the New Testament. Only slowly did monastic communities adopt formal vows,
beginning with the actual oath of St. Benedict and culminating in
the full-blown vows of the Gregorian and scholastic church under

Innocent III. The church obliged all religious to take the solemn vows of poverty, chastity, and obedience—the evangelical counsels.

Soon, however, new expressions of religious life began to emerge under the inspiration of the Holy Spirit. This was true among many of the Third Orders affiliated with the male mendicant communities. These communities found it more practical to take simple (or temporary) rather than solemn (or permanent) vows, freeing them from many of the more monastic obligations. This was true especially of the new sisterhoods who did not wish to be confined by the more strict monastic enclosure, or cloister, so they could be free to minister to the needs of the people. It was, indeed, a novel idea for sisterhoods in this period of the church. In times past communities with temporary vows were given an almost second-class status among religious institutes, but today they are viewed equally with institutes of permanent vows by canon law. This process went on for literally hundreds of years, thus manifesting how long this urging of the Spirit actually takes to unfold in the canonical structure of the church.

Next came the communities that expressed the evangelical counsels with a sacred commitment other than vows. These groups came to be called "Societies of the Apostolic Life." Again, this kind of commitment freed the communities from some of the more particularly intense expressions inherent in formal religious life, thus enabling the group more freely to engage in the apostolic work around which they were formed. Today, these groups resemble many of those classified as religious institutes, but actually constitute a classification unto themselves because of their unique call. Again, the new canon law does not view them as "second-class" religious communities, but as a group unto themselves with a unique and equally important call.

Also worth noting are the secular institutes. In these groups individuals privately vow the evangelical counsels without actually living in community. Thus, they live in the world without being of it. They have no habit, no cloister, no daily communal prayer. In this they are much like the associations of the faithful called "secular orders." Yet, unlike the secular orders, they actually vow poverty, chastity, and obedience. Unlike religious orders or societies of the apostolic life, they do not publicly vow or commit the evangelical counsels within an intentional community. Nor are they necessarily attached to a religious community. They are unique and are a reality unto themselves. At first they created many questions among the faithful in the church, but today they are viewed as a legitimate expression of the consecrated life.

It would also be good to mention the new provision in canon law for the ancient Christian expressions of consecrated virgin and anchorite or anchoress. These individuals also profess the evangelical counsels without actually joining a community. They do so through a "sacred bond" rather than through a public vow. Yet they are not actually members of a community. They may, especially the anchorites, "colonize" in a way similar to the early hermit colonies of the desert. All are individually under their bishop. This novel expression of the new canon law again indicates the willingness of the church legally to incorporate new expressions of the Spirit that are based on sound tradition and experience.

All of this only serves to point out that religious or monastic life is not static. It is alive even as the church is alive. It breathes with the very breath of God, the Holy Spirit. Spirits are tested and discerned through the apostolic structure of the church, but the genuine work of the Spirit keeps new communities constantly emerging through the concrete realities of the church and the vision of courageous founders and foundresses. Thus, the canonical realities of vows and commitments will always be developing. No one legal code will ever cover all the possibilities of the Spirit. New codes will constantly be devised to accommodate and define the working of the Holy Spirit, but just as soon as one code is passed, the Spirit will undoubtedly move on to something yet new, building solidly and surely on what has come before. Thus, a constant creative process of growth and definition is at work between the apostolic and charismatic dimensions of the church. Sometimes this involves creative tension, but any work of the Spirit is always done in union with the apostolic structure of the church.

It is with this creative process in mind that the new code of canon law allows for new expressions of religious life. Since they would be new, they cannot be defined; they can only be allowed for. Presumably, they would fulfill all of the requirements of religious life established by older expressions, but simply would not fit neatly into any existing expression or category.

They must be discerned by competent church authority so as to "test the spirits." In this case, the final authority is Rome. All local bishops, however, are to be alert to and sensitive to new forms raised up by the Spirit in their dioceses, so as to give them all the support they need from the church.

It is here, among other places, that the "covenant promise" might eventually be adopted by formal canon law. It might well serve to provide a more biblical language and content of commitment to new expressions of community. The covenant promise would be similar to the oath of the first cenobitic, monastic communities, or to the "other sacred bonds" of societies of the apostolic life, yet without limiting the nature of the institute to either monasticism or apostolic work. These commitments could be an ideal expression for communities that include everything that has come before without, however, being included by any one of them exclusively. They would be old, yet new!

Of course, the covenant community could also fit nicely into the "Associations of the Faithful" category of the new canon law. In this category they would not be considered formally "religious" or as living a "consecrated" life in the church, but there is certainly nothing to prohibit them from covenanting the evangelical counsels while in this category with church approval. This is temporarily done as a matter of course for any newly forming religious community in the church. Usually, this temporary period lasts from seven to ten years.

There could be several advantages to this option. First, it would allow members of other religious communities to join without totally severing their ties to their original religious institute. Thus, it could conceivably break through canonical barriers while respecting canonical structures. Second, it would allow for temporary commitments without an agenda toward permanent commitment. This is impossible for formal institutes of consecrated life, even if they make a series of temporary commitments. It would not, however, rule out perpetual commitments for those who wish to make them. Thirdly, it avoids the status symbol of being a religious in the church. This is a very real way to return to the littleness of the first hermit-monks and friars, who sought only to decrease so that Jesus might increase. Many times consecration backfires against this original intent, so that simple covenants, recognized by the church within a "mere" association of the faithful, might actually better realize the original intention of the eremitical and monastic founders and foundresses of ancient time. Along this line, the covenant keeps the commitments of "core" and lay "associates" on the same level. It does not place the celibate core above the associates in the status of the church.

Of course, there are disadvantages that come with this lack of status: The celibates lose the wealth of accumulated canonical and formal guidance and definition offered by existing in the consecrated category. It is not so much a matter of grasping after status as it is simply finding the existing canonical slot into which one best fits. There is no doubt in my mind that many new communities can fit quite easily into existing canon law.

Finally, whether one chooses the publicly vowed or the covenant promise expression, the choice must come from the same fire that burned within Francis's heart nearly 800 years ago. No "security-plan" choice will do for the authentic Franciscan, who ardently burns within and passionately longs to embrace fully the Crucified Lover in a total abandonment of one's self-will. The Seraphic Order of the future will cross all canonical barriers, but will in no way seek to undermine the authority or authenticity of the church. No cunning game plan to outmaneuver the divine authority of the church can ever be called authentically Franciscan. In our decisions of communal commitment we must seek radically to lay down our life with Christ for the eternal salvation of our community, the entire Franciscan family, the church, and the entire world. This is the primary reason for the existence of the true Franciscan hermitage.

22

NEW COMMUNITIES
AND CHURCH AUTHORITY

꒰꒱

S t. Francis was zealous in his submission and obedience
to the pope of the Roman Catholic Church. He lived in
a time when many small communities were rising up and breaking
away from the church. Not unlike his own new community, they
all sought to live the gospel as purely as possible. Sometimes this
led them into conflict with worldly bishops and clergy, and in some
cases with Rome itself. This was true especially in the case of the
Waldenses and the Cathari. Unlike them, Francis sought to win the
church back to Christ by his unswerving humble service. In this
he found a great friend in the dedicated reforming Pope Innocent
III. This led Francis further to place his community under the direct
protection of Rome, believing that Jesus would always guide the
Franciscan community through his promised authority on earth in
the pope.

This special obedience to the pope was further encouraged
through the dynamic international vision of his new brotherhood.
The older monastic forms of government saw each local monastery
as an independent quasi-church, related directly to the local church.
They were not necessarily an international religous order ruled by
one common superior. They were a sort of loose-knit federation of
independent communities, each ruled by its own abbot. Their link
with the church was usually with their local bishop. Francis's vision
was more than local. It was international. The world was his cloister.
Therefore, his whole international brotherhood was ruled by one

common superior, whose authoritative link with the church was with the bishop of Rome, the pope of the universal church.

After the time of Cluny in the tenth to twelfth centuries, almost all new monastic reforms adopted a centralized form of government. Each monastery still enjoyed a great deal of traditional autonomy and was ruled by its own abbot, but there was one set of norms and customs they all adhered to, and there was even a general governmental chapter and sort of superior who ruled the entire order. This superior did not enjoy all of the power of the minister general of the nonmonastic religious orders owing to the greater autonomy of each monastery and abbot, but the centralization broadened the vision and government of the monasteries adopting the reforms beyond the realm of their own local abbot and bishop.

This led to the practice of "exemption," which meant that almost all local religious communities were exempt from the authority of the local bishop regarding the internal affairs of the community. The local bishop had authority only over the external ministries of the community, and even this was limited. In all internal affairs, and in most ministries, the new "orders" were directly subject to the pope. The pope, in turn, granted great privileges to these new communities, which gave them almost unlimited freedom to exercise their ministries anywhere in the Catholic world. These new orders were regarded as a sort of papal army, going forth to promote reform and to evangelize the world.

Today we face a time not unlike that of St. Francis. There are splinter lay groups breaking away from the church under the banner of living the gospel more purely. We have clergy and religious breaking away as well, some to the right and some to the left. The episcopal hierarchy of the church is under attack, and some bishops are themselves also breaking off to the right or the left instead of being squarely centered on the gospel of Jesus Christ as passed on to us through the apostolic tradition of the church. In the face of all this we have a reforming pope, John Paul II, who is aggressively trying to restore the church to the solid foundation of the apostles and prophets, while squarely facing the present global challenges and looking with courage and hope into the future. This present pope is not unlike the aggressive reforming pope of St. Francis's day, Innocent III.

I believe that today we again need a radical obedience like St. Francis's. Francis's concept of obedience went far beyond mere legal minimums. His was a spiritual obedience that freed him far more than an independence which seeks its own rights under the banner of freedom. He was obedient to every living creature for God's sake. He was respectful of all people because they bore the image of God. He viewed all religious and clergy as his superiors. He had a deep respect for all priests and bishops because of their place in celebrating the great sacrament of the body and blood of Christ in the Eucharist. He did all this despite their personal sins or shortcomings. Finally, he humbly submitted to the pope in a deep belief that Christ had promised the pope the authority to guide the church on earth and, empowered by the Holy Spirit, that the pope would keep her from grave error. In this way he loved both the orthodox and the heretical among the laity and the clergy, but he safeguarded his own soul and his own brotherhod from falling into the grave errors embraced by so many in his own day.

Today we need a similar obedience. Our present pope speaks out for orthodoxy all over the world, yet he does so in a way that squarely faces modern issues and answers the myriad of confusing questions with the timeless gospel of Jesus Christ. No other world leader, religious or secular, has spoken out so fearlessly to the issues of peace and social justice that threaten the very existence of our modern world. The issues are obvious: the threat of nuclear war, the deadly atrocity of abortion, and the tragedy of global hunger and poverty. No other religious leader or modern evangelist has spoken out to so many and told them that the answer to these grave external crises can be solved only by a deep internal conversion to Christ and a radical conversion of lifestyle according to the example of Christ.

Yet this pope often meets with so much resistence from the very clergy and religious who profess obedience to him This is true especially in America. There are certainly issues on which we do not all agree, and certainly we can find historical precedent for valid and properly executed theological dissent. Compared to the more grave problems that face our church and our world, these problems often seem trivial and pale. We need to stop bickering over the things on which we do not agree. The future of our church and our world depend upon it! If we spent our time doing the things the pope has called us to do, and on which we all agree, we would barely have time for our theological and ecclessiastical squabbles that take up so much of our precious energy and time.

I believe that today we need a true sense of obedience to the pope once again. Today's church and world desperately need a literal army of clergy and religious united with the pope in his bold proclamation of the good news of Jesus Christ to this troubled world.

This kind of united obedience has real spiritual power. I am not advocating a blind or mindless obedience that squelches all theological investigation or the right to a humble and respectful theological dissent. I am, however, advocating keeping the more primary issues that face the church and the world central. We need the power of heartfelt unity in these areas. The future of the world and the church depend on it.

Under today's new canon law, such obedience also places us in closer union with the local bishop than ever before. Even communities directly under the pope are no longer able to exercise their ministries with the rather carefree attitudes of earlier eras in church history. Today, even these pontifical communities must obediently submit almost all of their external ministries to the local bishop. A real sensitivity to the local church is required. Conversely, even communities of diocesan right, or those directly under a local bishop in both internal and external matters, are guaranteed by Rome that the local bishop must always keep the specific charism of the religious community in mind. He cannot do anything that would destroy their authentic charism established by the Holy Spirit. Consequently, more than in any other time of church history the religious of the church are called to work in union with the local bishop and diocesan clergy, while retaining a zealous obedience to the pope.

More than ever before the mind of today's church blends together into a creative integration the monastic link with the church through the local bishop and the "orders' " link with the church through the bishop of Rome. The pontifical community can no longer claim "exemption" to get around obedience to the authority of the local bishop, nor can the traditionally more monastic approach, or the approach of communities of diocesan right, keep a more localized community from a real obedience to Rome. There is now a creative tension and balance between the two approaches that manifests real integration and healthy development, which is the result of the ongoing move of the Holy Spirit in the church.

From all of this it is fair to conclude that, like St. Francis, our approach should not be one of eluding church authority. If Francis sought to be directly under obedience to the bishop of Rome, it was not with a view to getting around the local bishop. Francis's obedience to the local bishops of his day went beyond mere legal observance of church law and won the support of even the most callous prelates through his gospel humility. Likewise, his obedience to local authority, much less his humble respect and obedience before all peoples and creatures of the earth, in no way kept him from an obedience to the pope that far exceeded the church law of his own day. Francis exhibited an obedience that was an obedience born of the spirit of Christ. It was an obedience that built up the church as she brought the gospel of Jesus Christ into his world. More than ever before in history we are now called by the Spirit to do the same. As I have said before and say again: The future of our divided church and our trouble-stricken world depend on it.

There are two views concerning the relationship between church leadership and religious communities. Both are based on the Pauline ecclessiology that sees the church as being built "on the foundation of the apostles and prophets, with Christ Jesus as the cornerstone." In this the apostolic dimension of the ongoing structure is represented in the bishops, who are the successors to the apostles. Some would say the prophetic dimension is structurally represented through the wide and varied religious communities of the church. The question is: how do they relate?

One view would see the apostolic and religious structures as growing up side by side, in a kind of parallel cooperation with one another, being rooted into Christ through a mutual submission to the pope. This view sees the religious as a kind of "holy rebel" whose job it is constantly to call the apostolic church from the formalism and legalism that can so easily overtake any institution. Of course, this is done in ultimate submission to the pope, albeit with some reservations at times. In an attempt to support this concept one can look to the relationship between the more charismatic prophets of the Old Testament and the more institutional establishment of the Levitical priesthood. The priesthood was established through a visible and traceable lineage, or succession, while the prophets were raised up at random by the Spirit "who blows where he wills." You can also support this approach with an appeal to early monasticism. As Mohler says, monasticism is "a lay protest against encroaching sacerdotalism, placing personal holiness higher than ecclesiastical succession." It is true that the early hermits wandered off into the desert, opting to live apart from the established institution of the church and even the sacraments, rather than be forced to live in compromise because of the secularized state of both the church and the world. This was radical. It is said that when St. Benedict was living in a solitary cave he had to be reminded by a visiting priest that it was Easter! He obviously was not preoccupied by even the most important liturgical events of the diocesan church.

This does not mean that he was antichurch. He just was not aggressively concerned. The same attitude could be seen somewhat in the early monastic mentality that saw each monstery as a quasi-church working alongside of, but separate from, the diocesan church. It can also be seen in some of the hermits and mystics of later centuries. Those who were actually antichurch could be seen breaking off into splinter groups who sacrificed the more primary principle of the unity of Christ's church for a secondary issue of a prophetic nature. This could be seen with the charismatic Montanists of the early church, or the Waldenses of the time of St. Francis. Both called for good things, but they did so at the expense of a greater thing: the unity of the church. St. Francis stands as a prophetic reminder to all Christian prophets that good things can be accomplished without destroying greater things. The unity of the church must always be maintained. The way of division has been tried and it did not work.

The second model sees the apostolic and the prophetic as more entwined as they grow up from the root of Christ and the common trunk of the pope. As the abbot of Beuron said during an intervention at Vatican Council II, the pillars of St. Peter's Basilica in Rome could be said to represent the apostles, but in the niches carved in the pillars appear the statues of the founders of religious institutes. This view sees the apostolic call of the bishops and the prophetic call of the religious as irreversibly and intimately intertwined, much as a man and woman become one, or intertwined, in marriage.

In his book *Religious Life* Elio Gamberi says, "Authentic charisms never contradict the hierarchical function of the church whose magisterium and ministry do not tend to 'stifle the Spirit' but to 'test everything and retain what is good' (1 Thess. 5:19). The hierarchy is led by the Spirit himself, and its office cannot be reduced to simple administration." He goes on, "It is inadmissible to appeal to the charism to challenge the authority of the pope and bishops. . . . The charismatic characters, far from justifying a certain independence from the hierarchy or even a parallel activity, constitute a new title of dependence on ecclessiastical authority. This dependence is not paralyzing." He says this from a deep conviction that it is the Holy Spirit who, in fact, guides the apostolic authority of the church. He also sees the dependent obedience of Jesus to the Father as a type of the obedience of the religious to the church. By and large, the latter view is in keeping with the mind of the church. It is not, at first look, radical. It appears "safe." But we should remember that working with the Spirit inside a religious structure is also a risk. It cost Jesus his life!

Speaking of the ongoing development of new communities in the church, Pope Paul VI said in his encyclical *Evangelization in the Modern World*:

> In some regions they appear and develop, almost without exception, within the church, having solidarity with her life, being nourished by her teaching and united with her pastors. . . . In other regions, on the other hand, 'communaute's de base' come together in a spirit of bitter criticism of the church, which they are quick to stigmatize as 'institutional' and to which they set themselves up in opposition as charismatic communities. . . . The difference is already notable: the communities which by their spirit of opposition cut themselves off from the Church, and whose unity they wound, can well be called 'communaute's de base,' but in this case it is a strictly sociological name. They could not without misuse of terms, be called ecclesial 'communaute's de base,' even if, while being hostile to the hierarchy, they claim to remain within the unity of the Church. This name belongs to the other groups, those which come together within the Church in order to unite themselves to the Church and cause the Church to grow.

But we do face a modern dilemma: Vocations to the priesthood are down while interest in small lay communities is up. Despite a myriad of renewal and evangelization programs, the local parish church remains a place largely unrenewed, where nominal faith is common through lack of zeal among clergy and laity. Can we put the "new wine" of renewal into the old wineskin of the parish church and the celibate ordained priesthood? I would like to tell you that we could. There is nothing essentially wrong with the diocesan parish structure or the ordained priesthood. Ideally, parishes could become places of renewal, and the priests could be the apostle-prophets of this renewal. But the sad fact is that, by and large, they are not. I would like to say the answer is the miracle of God inspiring more men to the priesthood, but, at present, God is not. The average parish remains seemingly unrenewed.

In light of this, a combination of the above two views of relationship might be in order. Perhaps the religious community, and its lay associates, could become an expression of the "base communities" spoken of by Paul VI. With this, nonordained religious and lay leadership or ordained permanent deacons might take up the slack in the loss of ordained priestly vocations. As the parishes struggle to exist, and the small communities prosper, the base community might even prove to be the basic structure of the church in years to come. This is radical, but it might be necessary if the church is to survive. I am reminded of the "Rome prophecies" of the 1978 charismatic conference in Rome where in effect the word was, "Look around you. All you see will fall down." The implication was that the outer complexion of the church might radically change, while its essential ecclessiology remains the same for it is ordained by Jesus Christ.

Of course, what would help to mark these small communities as authentic would be their obedience to the pope and bishops of the church, as well as to their ordained ministers, the priests and the deacons. This is what keeps even the base-community model squarely within the church.

Perhaps a reexamination of the Celtic monastic model might help us as we face this dilemma today. The Roman diocesan structure did not work, so the Celts simply used another. This other structure was monastic. Instead of the basic structure of the church being the parish, they saw that structure as the "base community" of the monastery. The monastery itself was made up of a community of monks, a community of nuns, and a community of celibate and married lay people. It was a veritable prayer town. A village to the glory of God! Because they were thus able to adapt their structures to the signs of the times and the existential wind of the Spirit, Catholic Christianity survived and flourished in the land of the Celts for centuries.

Notice that the Celtic model does not question the essential role of the bishops and the pope as successors to the apostles and St. Peter. It questioned only the local parish model and the model of diocesan authority. The Celts organized their church along monastic lines that were structured according to the local clan, or tribe, rather than trying to superimpose an artificial structure that would not really work in their land. But the role of the bishop and the pope remained intact. It must be asked: Is the parish structure God-breathed? Or is it the episcopal structure we see as divinely ordained? The parish structure can change, but the essential episcopal structure cannot. Otherwise, we have destroyed apostolic succession. The Celts then viewed the monastery as the local parish and diocesan seat, with the bishop many times being a monk of the monastery.

Notice, too, that the bishop and the abbot were not always the same person, mainifesting a healthy balance between the apostolic authority of the diocesan bishop and the prophetic authority of the abbot of the religious community. Granted, this might have manifested a different style of bishop, but it did not change any of the essential dimensions of the episcopal character. If anything, it enhanced an appreciation for the unique role of both. They worked together. When this did not work out, it was usually due to other more liturgical issues, such as the date of Easter or the style of clerical tonsure, and it usually involved bishops faced by the missionary St. Columban when he established monasteries in continental Europe. Even in these cases Columban appealed to and submitted to the authority of the pope as well as to his brother abbots. It cannot be said that Celtic monasticism was anti-Roman Catholic.

Today this might mean that local base Christian communities would be shepherded by clerical religious or lay leaders, who themselves would be ordained or appointed by the bishop. This would require that the bishop be quite sensitive to this new kind of community. It might even mean that he live in one, exercising his apostolic authority when necessary, but actually living in union with the base-community leadership in more domestic matters. I would point out that this leadership might be lay in character, and like St. Brigid or St. Hilda of old, it might be female. This, of course, presupposes that any leadership would be orthodox and obedient to church authority in the exercise of the church's sacred ministry.

This would not be unlike a provincial of a religious community living in a local community where he or she is not local superior. The provincial is over the local minister in all matters of provincial authority, but in many domestic and local affairs he or she cooperates fully with, and actually lives under, a local superior. Canon law even provides for the reality of a religious who is also a bishop. This has happened in various legitimate ways in the past. I suppose God could do it again!

I do not see this as supporting the two-parallel-trunks theory of relationship between the episcopal and the religious authority of the church. I see it as more in line with the one-column theory, where the column is adorned with the statues of many religious founders and foundresses. I do not see it, however, as a blind acceptance of the status-quo parish structures of the Western church. I believe we must stay in radical union with the primary structure of the pope and the bishops of the Roman Catholic Church, but I also believe we must at least consider alternate secondary structures if that church is to survive.

Perhaps a third model should be considered. Not unlike the "parallel-trunk" theory, I would see the double dimension of apostolic and prophetic as rising up side by side. But like the "one-column" theory, these must be connected together at every step, reaching across the space between them to form a sort of ladder leading to heaven. It is this ladder which enables God's little ones to climb to the heavens through the graces of the church. If the two parallel trunks are not seen as unique and different, even somewhat separate from one another, the ladder cannot be built. Also, if these two trunks are not connected at every development they will fall apart from each other and do not provide the proper steps on the ladder which enable the faithful to climb unto the heights of spirituality. Like all the gifts of the Spirit to the church, the religious and diocesan structures must be separate and unique, but also very tangibly connected.

A natural unfolding of this basic communization process in the church is the slow but sure transformation of the parish itself. As we have said before, the most ideal way is the simple renewal of the priesthood and the parish, but this way seems unlikely at the time of this writing—barring a major miracle from God. Of course, we continue to pray for such a miracle while we prepare alternative structures based on the tradition of the past and the experience of the present. The more probable way of transformation is simply to fill the gap left by the shortage of priests with ordained permanent deacons or appointed lay ministers of the Word and the Eucharist, or lay eucharistic ministers. Also, the division of the large parish into small groups through programs like "Renew" is a way of building basic Christian community into the parish itself. However, this still runs the danger of forming a small group according to a superficial plan or program rather than through individuals called mutually by the same Spirit. The traditional religious community could be an active core group in helping with this process. New religious communities raised up by the Spirit are a contemporary expression of new charism, while renewed older communities are an expression of developing charism. Both are good. This model is probably more in line with the mind of the church, is less threatening to most of the laity, and is therefore the most likely to succeed.

Another aspect of this consideration of new communities in the church is the apparent need for those of like heart and mind to gather together in small groups or communities before spreading out to evangelize both the church and the world. There are presently two contrasting, but complementary, views of the model we should use for this entire process of evangelization. The first model compares those who are "renewed" to leaven in the dough of the institutional structures of the church. Thus it sees renewal as an almost invisible, catalytic process in the church where existing structures and communities are renewed and kept from falling flat. The second model sees the need for those of renewed hearts and minds to gather together in groups or communities, either old or new, before going out to spread the good news of this renewal in the Spirit of Jesus Christ throughout the church and the world. This view recognizes the inability for even renewed Christians to maintain strength and refreshment in the Spirit while living alone in the desert of seemingly unrenewed structures. It recognizes our human weakness and our need for ongoing human channels of charismatic renewal in the Spirit.

The second model is really more scriptural and in union with the mind of the Catholic Church. This model goes back primarily to the words of Jesus and the experience of the early church. Jesus told them, "Remain [in Jerusalem] until you are clothed with power from on high . . . then you are to be witnesses in Jerusalem, throughout Judea and Samaria, yes, even to the ends of the earth." And before this power of the Holy Spirit came upon them they were first "gathered in one place" in "constant prayer." This experience was strengthened as they "were of one heart and mind as a community of believers" where "everything was held in common." From this community they ventured forth to give witness and to preach the good news of Jesus Christ. This happened primarily in Jerusalem with the religious structures of their day. "They went to the temple area together every day, while in their homes they broke bread. With exultant and sincere hearts they took their meals in common, praising God and winning the approval of all the people. Day by day the Lord added to their number those who were being saved."

Because of this scriptural example, the church has seen the need for those moved by the Spirit to gather together in new communities for mutual edification before venturing forth to evangelize those within the existing religious structures of the church, and reaching out from there to the ends of the earth. The church fathers viewed the renewing action of the Spirit as a constant process in the church, and the establishment of new communities and associations is a constant process. Each age has seen the establishment of new communities where people impelled by the Holy Spirit in similar ways gather together for the sake of mutual edification, which in turn strengthens the entire church and all the world.

> These latter communities will be a place of evangelization, for the benefit of bigger communities, especially the individual churches. And, as we said at the end of the last Synod, they will be a hope for the universal church to the extent:

- that they seek their nourishment in the Word of God and do not allow themselves to be ensnared by political polarization or fashionable ideologies, which are ready to exploit their immense human potential;

- that they avoid the ever-present temptation of systematic protest and a hypercritical attitude, under the pretext of authenticity and a spirit of collaboration;

- that they remain firmly attached to the local church in which they are inserted, and to the universal church, thus avoiding the very real danger of becoming isolated within themselves, then of believing themselves to be the only authentic church of Christ, and hence of condemning the other ecclesial communities;

- that they maintain a sincere communion with the pastors whom the Lord gives to his church, and with the Magisterium which the Spirit of Christ has entrusted to these pastors;

- that they never look on themselves as the sole beneficiaries or sole agents of evangelization—or even the only depositories of the gospel—but, being aware that the church is much more vast and diversified, accept the fact that this church becomes incarnate in other ways than through themselves;

- that they constantly grow in missionary consciousness, fervor, commitment, and zeal;

- that they show themselves to be universal in all things and never sectarian.

On these conditions, which are certainly demanding but also uplifting, the ecclesial *communautés de base* will correspond to their most fundamental vocation; as hearers of the gospel which is proclaimed to them and privileged beneficiaries of evangelization, they will soon become proclaimers of the gospel themselves. (Pope Paul VI, *Evangelization in the Modern World*)

Notice that it is the base of these new communities from which the older structures are renewed. Thus, the "leaven" is the new communities themselves, not always isolated individuals.

The problem we often face today is the tendency to opt for the "leaven-in-the-dough" model in an almost undue attempt to be in union with the existing structures of the church. In this we try not to overturn the "applecarts" of the existing institutional structures. Often, however, all that is accomplished is a compromise of the gospel and a quenching of the Holy Spirit in our own lives and, consequently, in the life of the entire church.

In this an isolated brother or sister will often stay within his or her particular community or institute in an attempt to be a leaven. While this is often good and is God's will, in other cases it causes an undue frustration on the part of the isolated brother or sister and upsets a whole existing community, turning them off to any possible expressions of genuine renewal. The isolated member often even loses his or her gift of the Spirit by having to stifle it continually to please his/her community members, and the entire church loses the benefit of the authentic charism from God.

The same thing can happen in parishes or in small groups. In order to keep the peace, charismatic individuals will silence their own gift in order to fit into the existing program. Prayer groups are kept in the background in "respectable" places, or small groups are formed superficially by an organizational plan or program, rather than by a genuine charism in which the Spirit calls certain individuals together for mutual edification. Ironically, it is the parish and the whole church that eventually suffer from this compromise which is apparently undertaken for the good of the church.

It might be good to recall the "second conversion" of Mother Theresa of Calcutta. She was an exemplary teaching sister of the Sisters of Loretto. Her life was good, but it was not radically on fire for the gospel. In the middle of a successful "career" she was called by God to something more radically "gospel." At age thirty-eight she obtained appropriate permission and began the "risk of love" among the poorest of the poor, which has culminated in the foundation of the Missionary Sisters of Charity, a new phenomenon of the love and the Spirit in the church. It was submitted to the church, but she did not compromise or back down from the radical gospel call she had received from God.

Or consider St. Anthony of Padua, who was a successful priest with the Canons Regular in Lisbon. He saw some of the members of the phenomenon of the Spirit raised up through the thirteenth century's St. Francis of Assisi. He, too, had a "second conversion" and joined the Franciscans, the Friars Minor. This was no doubt a difficult decision, but because of it the church gained a great saint.

23

THE PROBLEMS
OF SMALL COMMUNITY

☙

Despite the many advantages and encouragements to
small communities within the church, there still exists
many almost insurmountable problems to living within one, much
less founding one. After having lived in a small eremitical community for almost ten years, I now, half laughing and half crying,
tell people they have to be a masochist to *want* to start a new community in the church! There are inherent problems within and
without. The problems would be insurmountable without the gift
of grace, and even then it takes sheer faith to believe that "nothing
is impossible with God." Ultimately, the founding of a new community is the work of the Spirit. "If the Lord does not build the
house, in vain do the builders labor." If God is not really calling
you to this task, I beg you for your own good, do not do it! It can
be too painful.

First, there is the problem of community itself. A recent sociological study done for an established Franciscan community revealed some odd, disheartening facts. American Catholic people
simply do not want what is generally offered by Franciscan community. The problem? Individualistic attitudes! American candidates have not only an unhealthy individualism, but an unhealthy
individualistic approach to life in general. This makes community
life next to impossible. Despite our overabundance of talk about
Christian community, very few actually want to live it. We want
what we want when we want it. Most of us do not want to sacrifice

our personal freedom for the sake of community. A loose-knit parish life with few responsibilities or restrictions is one thing. Intentional religious community is quite another.

Second: Despite our abundant talk against institutionalization and clericalism, most candidates want the "professional" security of an "IBM-like" approach to spirituality, community, and ministry. Small communities, by their very nature, require an individual to use a great deal of undirected time creatively. Also economics alone sometimes dictate that one person will wear many hats. This often rules out highly specialized job opportunities, such as an ordination that requires years out of the community and tens of thousands of dollars. These professional pursuits are often not possible in small communities, especially those dedicated more intentionally to eremitism and itinerary.

As for clericalism: I recall a brother coming into our community. He listened to my classes on Franciscan spiritually and history for several months. Then one day he said, "Why should I listen to you? You are not a priest. You haven't been to seminary!" No matter that I had spent years studying on my own as a layman. No matter that I was generally well respected by Franciscan scholars regarding my opinions. All he knew was that I had not "been through the system." No doubt, the "system" is a safeguard against some error, and the priesthood is a commendable, ordained ministry. No doubt this brother had some justification for his views. But he did represent an attitude that made a small community patterned on ancient eremitical and early Franciscan values very difficult. My experience is that his attitude is very common. It has been said that the average Catholic would rather follow a fourth-rate priest than a first-rate layman.

Formation of new members is also a real problem for a small community. This is because each formed member has so many existent responsibilities that giving new members the time they deserve is next to impossible. Formation is almost a full-time job. In the typical small community it is part-time at best. There is the option of "farming out" the novices to shared novitiates. This can work well for more typical expressions. But for an expression of religious life as unique as Franciscan eremitism, you run a high risk of forming the individual into the very lifestyle you are trying to avoid.

The Franciscan dimension of the small eremitical community makes this all the more difficult. Ironically, since Franciscanism is based primarily on the gospel, it can appear to be "everywhere, but nowhere." While this works well as a mystical theology about God, it is a bit illusive for the description of a community! Since the community is an integration of solitude and community, contemplation and action, it can appear to be a little of both, but not really either. Other traditions might emphasize one or the other, but Franciscanism is usually an integration of both, all, or many, which makes it more difficult to define. While this works out quite well for some integrated individuals, for many or most it brings real confusion. This is an inherent tension, or problem, in Franciscan eremitism. It is our strength. It is also our weakness.

This confusion is often compounded the more integrated the community becomes. The Little Portion, for instance, has a highly integrated vision. It includes religious and seculars, celibate and married, men and women. It also integrates the hermitage with community, contemplation and action, the charismatic with the traditional, just to name the major points of integration. Each unique dimension is well defined, but the goal of proper integration is always kept in mind. While this vision seems very simple to me, and is based squarely on the gospels, the early church, and the witness of ancient eremitical and early Franciscan traditions, it is very confusing to many if not most of our observers. This has been and remains a major challenge for our community.

Of course, there are the many other problems that face a community such as ours. We emphasize prayer in a world of workaholics. We emphasize poverty in a world of rampant materialism. We emphasize obedience in a world of self-indulgent "freedom." We emphasize chastity in a world where sexual promiscuity is the norm. Our silence is a problem for those who are used to the constant noise, and solitude is a problem for those who are used to the rush of the crowd. Likewise, community is a problem for the rugged individualist. We live in a world where so many Christian values have broken down that it is hard enough to live the life of a normal Christian, much less the life of a Franciscan hermit or monk.

With all these challenges and seemingly insurmountable problems, it has been important for me to hang on to the prophecy of St. Bonaventure concerning the Seraphic Order and the "contemplative church of the future." I am well aware that the Spirit has raised up small eremitical communities much like ours throughout the church. They are not all Franciscan. Some are Benedictine, some are Carmelite, some are Dominican. Others do not even fit within an older religious family. Some even exist outside of the structure of Roman Catholicism. Yet, all are raised up by the Spirit to essentially the same semieremitical pattern of contemplative community life.

It is to this overall Seraphic Order I feel I really belong! Though these communities are not formally united, I know for a fact that we are united in the Spirit. Though some are not even formally established in the church, I know they are established by Christ through the power of the Holy Spirit. It was to this "order" that St. Francis ultimately belonged according to St. Bonaventure. This order spans space and time to give a very real security and stability to the small semieremitical communities that struggle to stay alive today. I believe that if we all tap into the strength of this greater order we will survive and, if the prophecy is correct, will prove to be a great prophetic witness as the church moves on to become the "contemplative church of the future."

24

MARRIED MONKS

෧

A long with the whole phenomenon of the Spirit raising up small eremitical prayer communities of celibates is the fact that many married couples are hearing a compelling call to the contemplative/monastic life. This too, I believe, is a phenomenon of the Spirit working within the church. It has its own unique set of problems and challenges, but it is still very much related to the move of the Spirit calling celibates to a similar life.

From history we can see that this phenomenon is not entirely new. Husbands and wives often felt the call to a more radical Christian life among the early Christian ascetics. We also know that some couples felt the call to the solitude of the desert. Also, many couples joined themselves to the "order" of penitents in order more radically to follow Christ. In most of these cases, abstinence from sexual activity was the norm. They lived as brother and sister in continent marriages. While this can be problematic to contemporary theology of marriage, and the goodness of the sexual act in Christian marriage, it cannot be denied that this arrangement gave birth to many saints.

However, as time went on sexual abstinence was not the norm for those seeking a more "monastic" life as married couples. The Celtic model of monasticism included not only monks and nuns living together in a double monastery, but also families. It is interesting to note that these monastic couples, and even their children, were considered monks and nuns and full members of the monastic village. Of course, the class of penitents continued on in the church as a state of life neither monastic nor secular, but as something unique unto itself. It too, began to allow sexual expression for the married members. This penitential order developed into what we now call "oblates" of monasteries, or "third orders" associated with the mendicant orders. New congregations of subsequent generations also attracted families to share in their communal life and work.

With the passing of time these associate families took on a more "secular" approach to their life, and became separated from the domestic communal lives of the religious celibate members of their communities. In some ways this was good, for it more clearly defined the unique role of both celibate and married members of particular spiritual families. In other ways it was bad, for it divided one from the other and gave rise to a subtle class system of superior and inferior states of life.

I suppose it could be argued that the concept of a "married monk" is a misnomer. The word "monk" implies companionship and community. But this argument also applies to the cenobitical monk, who no longer lives as a hermit, but in community with others. It is now proper to call the cenobite a monk, so I suppose the concept of a married monk is, from this perspective at least, possible.

I think this "monasticism" is more a matter of the heart and of domestic lifestyle than of canonical states. I know many married couples who are far more contemplative than some of the workaholics I have encountered in contemplative houses. Likewise, I know some couples who maintain a genuine spirit of silence and prayer in their houses that far surpasses some of the official "houses of prayer" I have visited. It is not impossible for the family to embrace this lifestyle, complete with formal prayer, times for silence and solitude, and appropriate apostolic ministry.

The question of children rightly comes up when considering this concept of married monks. Will not such a lifestyle "warp" children? Is not such silence and discipline unhealthy for normal kids?

First, it must be admitted that for a family to change abruptly from the typical American scene to a monastic setting will cause domestic and psychological problems. The kids simply will not understand why something that was domestically normal yesterday is suddenly taboo today. But the same logic applies to a couple who change from a non-Christian lifestyle to a Christian life. The kids will be confused. In either case sensitivity and care will have to be used to explain such a radical domestic change. It does not always follow that there should be no change at all.

Secondly, for children who are raised in such an environment, this way of life is itself completely normal. In fact, many children have a high sensitivity and apptitude to such spirituality. The example of healthy children raised in Buddist monasteries shows that such a pattern is possible. Of course, Christian monasticism is filled with examples of perfectly normal individuals raised in a monastery. Some even went on to become saints! The Protestant tradition gives us the Mennonites, the Amish, the Quakers, and the Hutterites who live a nearly "monastic" life as families. Of course, the birth of Christian monasticism itself came from the Jewish example of the Essenes, who included men, women, and children in their communities.

In all this, however, care must be taken not to isolate the children from the real world, be it ever so worldly and filled with sin. Married monastaries could rightly *insulate* a child from the cold, hard realities of a sinful world, but it should not *isolate* them. One protects, the other simply hides.

Along with this is the consideration of the natural and healthy play needed by a child. This play is *noisy!* As in Eastern monasteries, this play could sometimes be directed into Christian Yoga and developmental games quite compatible with the contemplative environment. In this the married monastery stands in prophetic contrast to the noisy chaos of many American Christian households. Personally, I do not think this chaos is always good. But I do think some loud play is important. In this, care should be taken to provide sufficient time and space for such activities.

I write this from the perspective of a celibate hermitage community that would not welcome such intrusion on a daily basis. We do enjoy the presence of children as guests, but I do not think it would be good as a daily reality. Because of this, I believe the married monks should live in their own area, close enough to the celibates to retain real communal ties, but far enough away environmentally to protect the uniqueness of each call. I would point out, however, that even we sober celibates have a need to let off a little steam about once a week in recreation, and would do well to be more faithful and pay more attention to this healthy and normal human need.

Even with these observations and cautions, I believe God is calling many to this "married monasticism," and that the Lord desires to raise up "monastic villages." These villages have to be powerful centers of prayer. They are to manifest an alternative radical Christianity to a society, both religious and secular, grown lukewarm, cold, and compromised. I believe the time is now to take the risk to "sell all and follow me," Christ the Lord. It was done by the early church in Jerusalem and it shook the whole world in the power of the Holy Spirit. It was done by a radical few in the reforms of subsequent generations. Can we be any less courageous today?

There is another important difference in dynamics between the celibate and married monks. This has to do with the hierarchy of priorities in communal structure itself. I teach according to the following diagram:

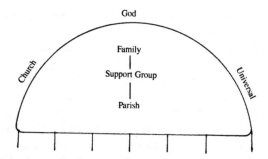

According to this diagram, God is our first priority. After that comes the church, but the church is not a particular expression of Christian life. It includes every aspect of being Christian. Within the church, the nuclear family is the primary expression of community. All of us, celibate or married, come first from the family community. Next comes the support group, or intentional community. This might be a base community, a covenant community, or a religious community. These smaller support communities network together in the typical large parish or diocesan structures of the church. The parish and diocese is usually too large to be a real support for ongoing personal relationships in Christ, but it does become a support for the support groups. From this whole church—family, support group, parish, and diocese—the world is evangelized.

It is on the level of family and support group that there exists a real difference between celibates and the married. For the celibate the religious community becomes the primary "family." From this other secondary support groups might be entered into, such as renewal groups or even covenant communities. For the married monks the nuclear family will always remain the primary expression of community. The monastic community family will always be secondary. Thus, for the celibate monk the monastic family is primary. For the married monk it is secondary.

This is an important and substantial difference. It affects the way obedience, for example, is lived out. For the married monk, the communal obedience will always be secondary to the more primary mutual obedience of husband and wife. For the celibate, communal obedience is second only to individual conscience. Poverty, likewise, is affected by the more primary role of the nuclear family, as contrasted to the more free responsibility of the individual celibate. In both of these, the community is more removed as a priority for the couples than it is for the celibates. This is all right. It is proper. Chastity, of course, is lived out in a different way for a married couple than for a celibate. There are only a few differences that must be recognized and respected if celibate and married monks are to associate in some kind of community together.

Barring the more obvious differences between the way celibates and marrieds live out the monastic or eremitical life, the common inspiration and implementation of the life is shared substantially. This common ground was, at first, recognized by the church. Then differences were defined, and concentration on the differences blinded most of us to the more numerous similarities. Diversity became fragmentation. Fragmentation concluded in division. Today we face the challenge of reuniting this overall monastic call that goes forth to all Christians. There will still be difficulties. There will still be definition of difference. But I pray this will never again degenerate into the division that stifles the Spirit of God and hinders our effectiveness in bringing the full and radical gospel of Jesus Christ to all the world.

Perhaps it would be good to conclude this chapter with a quote from St. John Chrysostom's (c. 349–407) work on monastic life:

> The Holy Scriptures do not know any distinctions. They enjoin that all lead the life of monks even if they are married. Listen to what Paul says (and when I say Paul, I say also Christ) in writing to married men who have children. He demands from them the same rigorous observance as that demanded from monks. He removes all luxury in their dress and food in writing: "Women are to pray, decently attired, adorning themselves with modesty and restraint, not with braided hair, gold, pearls, or expensive clothing, but with good deeds as befits women who make profession of

worshiping God" (1 Tim. 2:9). And again: "She who gives herself up to pleasure is dead while she is still alive" (1 Tim. 6:8). And again: "If then we have something with which we can nourish and clothe ourselves, let us be content with it" (1 Tim. 6:8). What could we demand more of from the monks?

Conclusion

❧

W e are faced with many serious questions. Does community really work anymore? Is monastic and Franciscan eremitism irrelevant to our modern world? Can the modern church survive without them?

This book has been an attempt to look at monastic eremitical and Franciscan origins, and use some of the precedents found in this communal history to come up with some new integrations. We have looked at many external forms and tried to point out a pluriformity that is rooted squarely in tradition and orthodoxy. I hope we have also been able to capture the spirit of the overall evolution, development, and process of what we call eremitism. Through all this I hope we have shed some light on how both monastic and Franciscan eremitism can remain vitally important to the church in the modern world.

At the time of this writing, I am not sure if the concept of Christian community really works in the U.S. At the same time, I am convinced that the church in America will not really survive without developing, embracing, and encouraging new forms of religious and lay community. I have heard the countless complaints about typical parish life, yet I have seen a seemingly endless stream of spiritual dreamers come through my new Franciscan hermitage. From the reports of other new religious communities, our experience at Little Portion is not unique. The failure of new religious communities to keep members is, in fact, normal in America. In this we are no more successful than the older communities. Covenant communities of lay people enjoy a little more success, but any form of community that requires commitment is immediately facing a challenge in a modern world where commitment is hard to find. Personally, I am at a bit of an impasse. I am watching, waiting, and holding fast to the vision.

Ultimately the call to these new forms of Franciscan or monastic eremitism is prophetic. In this, those of us called must be made of some pretty tough stuff. We must be able to endure the loneliness, the heartache, even the rejection of staying true to the call. We do this not out of some kind of masochism or a messianic complex. We do this out of hope and assurance. Assurance that God has called us, and hope that if we do respond, we will in fact experience his companionship. We also do this in the hope that our solitary witness today may prompt many to respond to God's call tomorrow. That call will undoubtedly involve both action and prayers, solitude and community. In this, the full historic vision of monastic and Franciscan eremitism cannot help but play an important, albeit a small, part.

References

❧

Chapter 1. The Tradition of the Desert Fathers

Allchin, A. M. *Solitude and Communion.* Fairacres, Oxford: S.I.G. Press, 1975. Chaps. 1, 2, and 3.

Chadwick, Owen. *John Cassian.* Cambridge: Cambridge University Press, 1968. Chap. 2.

Chitty, Derwas J. *The Desert a City.* Crestwood, NY: St. Vladimir's Seminary Press, 1966.

Fry, Timothy, O. S. B. *The Rule of St. Benedict in Latin and English with Notes.* Collegeville, MN: Liturgical Press, 1980. Introduction, "Historical Orientation."

Isabell, Damien, O. F. M. *Workbook for Franciscan Studies.* Chicago: Franciscan Herald Press, 1979. Pp. 320–26.

McCarren, Charles, O. F. M. Cap. "The Desert Father Pattern and the Franciscan Hermitage." Eremetical Conference II, Graymoor, N.Y., 1984.

Mohler, James A., S. J. *The Heresy of Monasticism.* Staten Island, NY: Society of St. Paul, 1971. Chap. 4.

Palladius, Saint. *Ancient Christian Writers.* Vol. 34. *The Lausiac History.* New York: Paulist Press, 1964.

Skudlarek, William, O. S. B. *The Continuing Quest for God.* Collegeville, MN: Liturgical Press, 1982. Chaps. 3 and 4.

Chapter 2. Early Ascetics, Virgins, and Itinerant Prophets

Mohler, James A., S. J. *The Heresy of Monasticism.* Staten Island, NY: Society of St. Paul, 1971. Chap. 2.

Skudlarek, William, O. S. B. *The Continuing Quest for God.* Collegeville, MN: Liturgical Press, 1982. Chaps. 2 and 7.

Chapter 3. Celtic Monasticism

Bonaventure, Saint. *Collations on the Six Days*. Patterson, NJ: St. Anthony Guild Press, 1970. Chaps. 22:22.

Brooke, Christopher. *Monasteries of the World*. New York: Crescent Books, 1982. Chap. 3.

Brown, Raphael, *True Joy from Assisi*. Chicago: Franciscan Herald Press. 1978. Chap. 20.

Farmer, David Hugh. *Benedict's Disciples*. Leominster, Herefordshire. Fowler Wright Books, 1980. Chaps. 3 and 4.

Fry, Timothy, O, S. B. *The Rule of St. Benedict in Latin and English with Notes*. Collegeville, MN Liturgical Press, 1980.

McCarren, Charles, O. F. M. "Celtic Eremitism." Eremetical Conference II, Graymoor, N.Y., 1984.

Mohler, James A., S. J. *The Heresy of Monasticism*. Staten Island, NY: Society of St. Paul, 1971. Chap. 8.

Chapter 5. The Gregorian Reform

Allchin, A. M. *Solitude and Communion*. Fairacres, Oxford: S.I.G. Press, 1975. Chapters 1–5.

Lackner, Bede K., S. O., Cist. *The Eleventh-Century Background of Citeaux*. Washington, DC: Cistercian Publications, Consortium Press, 1972.

McCarren, Charles, O. F. M., Cap. "A Possible Dialogue between the Camaldolese and the Early Franciscans." Unpublished paper, 1983.

Robinson, Michael, O. F. M., Cap. "St. Francis of Assisi and the Camaldolese Tradition. Unpublished paper, 1983.

Salmon, Dom Pierre, O. S. B. *The Abbot in Monastic Tradition*. Washington, DC: Cistercian Publications, Consortium Press, 1972. Chap. 6.

Chapter 6. The Penitential Movement

Pazelli, Raffaele, T. O. R. "Outline of the History and Spirituality of the Franciscan Penitential Movement." Unpublished paper, 1978.

Chapter 7. The Mendicants

Gutierrez, David, O. S. A. *The Augustinians in the Middle Ages 1256–1356*. Villanova, PA: Augustinian Historical Institute, 1984.

Martin, Thomas P., O. S. A. "From Hermit to Friar," *The Tagasten* Volume 29, Number 2. Villanova, Pa. Augustinian Friars, Province of St. Thomas of Villanova. 1983.

Oldfield, John J., O. A. R. "Recollect and Renewal within the Augustine Order," *The Tagasten* Volume 31, Number 1. Villanova, Pa. Augustinian Friars. Province of St. Thomas of Villanova. 1985.

Rano, Balbino, O. S. A. *History of the Order of St. Augustine.* Volume 1, Part 1, Chapter 1. Villanova, Pa. Augustinian Friars, Province of St. Thomas of Villanova. 1970.

Smet, Joachim O., Carm. *The Carmelites.* Darien, IL: Carmelite Spiritual Center, 1976.

Chapter 8. The Franciscan Hermitage

Brown, Raphael. *True Joy from Assisi.* Chicago: Franciscan Herald Press, 1978.

Dubois, Alberic. *Conversations in Umbria.* Chicago: Franciscan Herald Press, 1980.

Esser, Cajetan, O. F. M. *Origins of the Franciscan Order.* Chicago: Franciscan Herald Press, 1970.

Isabell, Damien, O. F. M. *Workbook for Franciscan Studies.* Chicago: Franciscan Herald Press, 1979. Pp. 277–84.

Merton, Thomas. *Contemplation in a World of Action: Franciscan Eremitism.* Garden City, NY: Image Books, 1973. Part 2, Chap. 3.

Mrozinski, Ronald M., O. F. M. *Franciscan Prayer Life.* Chicago: Franciscan Herald Press, 1981.

Chapter 11. Tertiaries

Aspurz, Lazaro de, O. F. M. Cap. *Franciscan History.* Chicago: Franciscan Herald Press, 1983.

Habig, Marion, O. F. M. *The Franciscan Book of Saints.* Chicago: Franciscan Herald Press, 1979.

Chapter 12. A Universal Seraphic Order

Bonaventure, Saint. *Collations on the Six Days.* Patterson, NJ: St. Anthony Guild Press, 1970. Chap. 22:22.

Brown, Raphael, O. F. M. *True Joy from Assisi.* Chicago: Franciscan Herald Press, 1978.

Chapter 13. Toward a New Franciscan Eremitism

Bonaventure, Saint. *Collations On the Six Days.* Patterson, NJ: St. Anthony Guild Press, 1970 Chap. 22:22.

Brown, Raphael, O. F. M. *True Joy from Assisi.* Chicago: Franciscan Herald Press, 1978. Chap. 20.

Esser, Cajetan, O. F. M. *Origins of the Franciscan Order.* Chicago: Franciscan Herald Press, 1980.

Chapter 14. Toward a Universal Monasticism

Bonaventure, Saint. *Collations on the Six Days*. Chapter 22:22. Patterson, New Jersey. St. Anthony Guild Press. 1970.

Esser, Cajetan, O. F. M. *Origins of the Franciscan Order*. Chicago: Franciscan Herald Press, 1980.

Mohler, James A., S. J. *The Heresy of Monasticism*. Staten Island, NY: Society of St. Paul, 1971.

Salmon, Dom Pierre, O. S. B. *The Abbot in Monastic Tradition*. Washington, DC: Cistercian Publications, Consortium Press, 1972.

Chapter 15. The Itinerant Ideal

Aspurz, Lazaro de, O. F. M. Cap. *Franciscan History*. Chicago: Franciscan Herald Press, 1981.

Esser, Cajetan, O. F. M. *Origins of the Franciscan Order*. Chicago, Ill. Franciscan Herald Press. 1980. Chap. 2:1.

Mohler, James A., S. J. *The Heresy of Monasticism*. Staten Island, NY: Society of St. Paul, 1971.

Pazaelli, Raffaele, T. O. R. "Outline of the History and Spirituality of the Franciscan Penitential Movement." Unpublished paper, 1978.

Chapter 17. Integrating East and West

Bonaventure, Saint. *Mystical Opuscula: The Journey of the Mind to God*. Patterson, NJ: St. Anthony Guild Press, 1960. Chap. 7:4.

Bonaventure, Saint. *Mystical Opuscula: The Triple Way, or Love Enkindled*. Patterson, NJ: St. Anthony Guild Press, 1960. Chap. 3, F 11–13.

Brown, Raphael, O. F. M. *True Joy from Assisi*. Chap. 14, 23:2, Appendix D, p and q. Chicago: Franciscan Herald Press, 1978.

Johnston, William. *Christian Zen*. New York: Harper and Row, 1971.

Lossky, Vladimir. *The Mystical Theology of the Eastern Church*. Crestwood, NY: St. Vladmir's Seminary Press, 1976. Chaps. 2 and 11.

Maloney, George A., S. J. *The Mystic of Fire and Light*. Denville, NJ: Dimension Books, 1967.

Pennington, M. Basil, O. C. S. O., editor. *One Yet Two*. Kalamazoo, MI: Cistercian Publications, 1976.

Zander, Valentine. *St. Seraphim of Soroy*. Crestwood, NY: St. Vladmir's Seminary Press, 1975.

Chapter 18. Obedience

Esser, Cajetan, O. F. M. *Origins of the Franciscan Order*. Chicago, Ill. Franciscan Herald Press. 1980. Chap. 2.

Chapter 19. A Question of Leadership

Salmon, Dom Pierre, O. S. B. *The Abbot in Monastic Tradition.* Washington,
DC: Cistercian Publications, Consortium Press, 1972.
Vogue, Adalbert de. *Community and Abbot.* Kalamazoo, MI: Cistercian
Publications, 1978.

Chapter 20. The Habit

Esser, Cajetan, O. F. M. *Origins of the Franciscan Order.* Chicago: Fran-
ciscan Herald Press, 1980. Chap. 2.
Fry, Timothy, O. S. B. *The Rule of St. Benedict in Latin and English with
Notes.* Collegeville, MN: Liturgical Press, 1980.

Chapter 21. Vows and Promises

Fry, Timothy, O. S. B. *The Rule of St. Benedict in Latin and English with
Notes.* Collegeville, MN: Liturgical Press, 1980. Appendix 5.
Chadwick, Owen. *John Cassian.* Cambridge: Cambridge University Press,
1968.
Mohler, James A., S. J. *The Heresy of Monasticism.* Staten Island, NY: So-
ciety of St. Paul, 1971.

Chapter 24. Married Monks

Skudlarek, William, O. S. B. *The Continuing Quest for God.* Collegeville,
MN: Liturgical Press, 1982.
Mitchum, Carl. *The Families of St. Benedict: A Contemporary Adaptation
of Monastic Life.* Collegeville, MN: Liturgical Press. 1982. Pp. 257–67.
Mitchum, Marylee. *An Accidental Monk.* Cincinnati: St. Anthony Messenger
Press, 1976.